The Rise of
CHINA and INDIA
A New Asian Drama

The Rise of
CHINA and INDIA
A New Asian Drama

Lam Peng Er
Lim Tai Wei

East Asian Institute, National University of Singapore, Singapore

 World Scientific

NEW JERSEY · LONDON · SINGAPORE · BEIJING · SHANGHAI · HONG KONG · TAIPEI · CHENNAI

Published by

World Scientific Publishing Co. Pte. Ltd.

5 Toh Tuck Link, Singapore 596224

USA office: 27 Warren Street, Suite 401-402, Hackensack, NJ 07601

UK office: 57 Shelton Street, Covent Garden, London WC2H 9HE

British Library Cataloguing-in-Publication Data
A catalogue record for this book is available from the British Library.

THE RISE OF CHINA AND INDIA
A New Asian Drama

ISBN-13 978-981-4280-33-4
ISBN-10 981-4280-33-X

Typeset by Stallion Press
Email: enquiries@stallionpress.com

Printed in Singapore.

Acknowledgements

The genesis of this book was based on the Mahatma Gandhi–Daisaku Ikeda Peace Research Conference on *"The Rise of China and India: Towards a Harmonious Region?"* in August 2008. This conference was organized by the East Asian Institute (EAI), Singapore and generously sponsored by Lam Kin-chung Morning Sun Charity Fund and Dr Ho Hau Wong.

Besides our profound thanks to our sponsors, the editors are also grateful to Professor Wang Gungwu, Chairman of EAI, Professor Zheng Yongnian, Director of EAI and Professor John Wong, Director of Research at EAI for their kind support to bring this project into fruition. We extend our appreciation to the World Scientific editorial team for bringing this edited volume out in a timely manner.

Contents

Acknowledgements   v

Chapter 1   Introduction: China, India and the   1
            New Asian Drama
            Lam Peng Er and Lim Tai Wei

Chapter 2   The Rise of China: Conflict or Harmony   11
            in East Asia?
            Ding Dou

Chapter 3   Emerging India and China: Potentials   21
            and Constraints
            K. M. Seethi

Chapter 4   The Rise of China and India and Its   39
            Implications for Southeast Asia:
            A Philippine Perspective
            Noel M. Morada

Chapter 5   Negotiating the Rise of Asia — A Perspective   59
            from Malaysia's Relations with India
            and China
            Johan Saravanamuttu

Chapter 6   A Japanese Perspective on the Rise of China   79
             and India: Opportunities, Concerns,
             and Potential Threats
             Minoru Koide

Chapter 7   The Rise of China and India: Geo-political   99
             Narratives from the Singapore Perspective
             Lim Tai Wei

Chapter 8   The Rise of China and India and Its   127
             Implications for Southeast Asia:
             A Thai Perspective
             Prapat Thepchatree

Bibliography   147

Index   161

Chapter 1

Introduction: China, India and the New Asian Drama

Lam Peng Er and Lim Tai Wei

In 1968, Karl Gunnar Myrdal, a Swedish economist, politician and Nobel laureate wrote his landmark study *Asian Drama: An Inquiry into the Poverty of Nations*.[1] This work pessimistically analyzed the difficulties of development in South Asia and the widening gap between rich and poor nations, and concluded that the Asian drama could well turn out to be a tragedy. In the same year the *Asian Drama* was published, India was mired in economic stagnation and Maoist China was in the throes of the self-inflicted Cultural Revolution. Few could have imagined from the vantage point of 1968 that barely four decades later a new and contrarian Asian Drama would unfold — the rise of China and India on the global stage. Both countries are emerging economic power houses, autonomous great powers in their respective regions, and are major civilizations. Indeed, they have exercised cultural "soft power" in Southeast Asia for more than a millennium. In 2008, China put on a spectacular display and a great feat of organization at the Beijing Summer Olympics and succeeded in stunning and wooing a global audience.

The importance of these two Asian giants can hardly be exaggerated. Combined, their population comprises more than a third of

---

[1] Karl Gunnar Myrdal, *Asian Drama: An Inquiry into the Poverty of Nations*, 3 Vols. (New York: Pantheon Books, 1968).

Table 1: Top 10 Countries: Economy

Country	GDP (PPP): US$
1. US	13,840,000,000,000
2. China	6,991,000,000,000
3. Japan	4,290,000,000,000
4. India	2,989,000,000,000
5. Germany	2,810,000,000,000
6. United Kingdom	2,137,000,000,000
7. Russia	2,088,000,000,000
8. France	2,047,000,000,000
9. Brazil	1,836,000,000,000
10. Italy	1,786,000,000,000

Note: Figures are 2007 estimated.
Source: Central Intelligence Agency, *World Factbook*, 4 September 2008.

humanity. The Chinese economy today is already the second largest in the world while India is ranked fourth according to PPP (purchasing power parity) calculations (Table 1). Even though both countries do not share the same regime types — India is an electoral democracy while China a nominally communist system — they have shifted away from stultifying central state planning and embraced market forces and reforms. In this regard, they are now enjoying considerably higher rates of economic growth which have helped to reduce mass poverty.

While India and China are by no means rich countries on a per capita basis, they are now undergoing a social and economic transformation including the rise of a significant urban middle class underpinned by mass consumerism. If these two countries were to maintain their present rate of economic growth, they could conceivably wipe out the scourge of poverty within a few decades time. But even then, they will at best become middle-income nations on a per capita basis given their gargantuan population size.

Moreover, China and India are political, technological and military heavyweights in their regions. China is a permanent five member of the United Nations Security Council while India is seeking a similar status in that global body. Both countries are nuclear powers. In 2005, Prime Minister Manmohan Singh and President George W. Bush signed a major atomic energy pact which allowed the transfer of Western technology and cheap atomic energy to India. Prime Minister Singh declared in September 2008: "We are on the verge of securing a new status in the global nuclear order".[2] In the same month, China conducted its first space walk and became the only third country after the US and Russia to send astronauts into space. In the following month, India successfully launched its first unmanned mission to the moon. Apparently, India plans to send a man to the moon by 2025.

Unlike Japan which is a one-legged economic giant, India and China are "complete" great powers in international politics not allied or the junior partner to any superpower, and underpinned by economic, military and cultural strength.

While India and China's rapid rise is indeed impressive, three caveats must be lodged. First, even though the ascendancy of both Asian giants is often stated in the same breath, we argue that there are considerable differences between them. Simply put, China still is ahead economically. Indeed, China has set a blistering pace in its economic development and India has yet to draw abreast with the former. Moreover, China has established an excellent physical infrastructure of roads, rails, bridges and airports, India has yet to match China in this dimension. However, India seemed to have leapfrogged from an agrarian nation to one with considerable expertise in computer software, and call centers. But India has not become a manufacturing hub of the world like China. In this regard, both nations have carved out their comparative advantage. Nevertheless, China and India, like other countries in the world, are confronted by a "once in a life time" global financial tsunami triggered by the US sub-prime mortgage crisis in 2008–09. If both countries can weather this economic crisis well, their role as emerging great economic powers appears secure.

---

[2] "Indian PM says nuclear deal to bring new status", Channel News Asia, 28 September 2008. Available at <http://www.channelnewsasia.com/stories/afp_asiapacirfic/print/378938/1/.html> (Accessed on 29 September 2008).

Second, both nations share the challenge of governing huge countries with significant ethnic minorities. Although the ethnic Han Chinese comprises 92 percent of China's population, the nation has 53 recognized minority groups who occupy large areas of the nation's land mass. Beijing has to deal with restive Tibetans and Muslim separatists in Xinjiang province. Similarly, India is a plural society differentiated by ethnicities, sub-cultures and the caste system. Besides the potential political fault lines between the Hindus and the Muslims, India is also confronted by a low intensity and yet troubling armed insurrection by the Maoist-inspired Naxalites in more than ten provinces. Both countries also have problematic neighbors. China may face the challenge of an imploding North Korean regime (which is nuclear armed) after the death of its dictator Kim Jong-il, a flood of refugees and instability in the Korean peninsula. India is bedeviled by an unstable Pakistan (another nuclear power). The mayhem in Mumbai where Pakistani-linked Jihadis terrorists struck at civilian targets in November 2008 poignantly reveals the vulnerability of India despite its ascendance as a great power.

Third, there are occasional setbacks to the good images of both countries. In 2008, China was rocked by a food scandal in which its milk products were contaminated by melamine which affected the health of at least 53,000 infants. Despite the considerable progress of China in many sectors, the milk fiasco poignantly shows that the country has a weak and inadequate regulatory system. Not surprisingly, the contamination of food produced in China has created disquiet in the export markets of the country. In the same year, a mob of Indian workers bludgeoned to death the head of the Indian operations of Graziano Transmissioni, an Italian manufacturer of car parts, who sacked them from a factory in a suburb of Delhi. In another incident the same year, the Tata industrial group which planned to build the world's cheapest car threatened to relocate the factory in West Bengal after political activists and farmers besieged the existing site. While both incidents in India may be dismissed as dramatic but isolated incidents, we wonder whether there is considerable ambivalence if not resistance towards industrialization among certain local governments, workers and farmers in that nation.

Notwithstanding these problems, India and China continue to enjoy rapid economic development. The industrialization of the US, Western Europe and Japan have created considerable socio-economic, political and environmental problems and tradeoffs in the past and, therefore, China and India's developmental problems and challenges are by no means unique. This observation is not an excuse to absolve the lack of proper regulation in certain cases by Chinese or Indian authorities but just an awareness how difficult it is to direct the Asian Drama from the poverty to the wealth of nations. Indeed, a precondition for human security and dignity is the eradication of poverty and both China and India are making progress in this area through rapid economic growth.

This book seeks to examine the views of indigenous scholars from China, India and Southeast Asia towards the rise of both giants on the Asian stage. We do not seek to impose any straight jacket orthodoxy in their mode of analysis and have purposefully allowed each scholar to pick his line of enquiry from a country perspective. The views of this book is, therefore, eclectic — a mirror of many views, some divergent, towards the rise of India and China. Indeed, this diversity of views reflects the uncertainty, different perceptions and values of many East and South Asian specialists as they watch the new Asian Drama unfolds. To use the analogy of critics, reviewers and spectators at a play with different tastes, experiences and expectations will naturally have different impressions of the on going Asian Drama with many more episodes to come.

Chapter Summaries

Ding Dou's opening chapter analyzes the rise of China from a Chinese perspective but using Western traditional international relations (IR) approaches: realism, liberal institutionalization and constructivism. He gives a succinct survey of the different schools of thought amongst Western IR scholars and tests them against Chinese nativist and indigenous worldviews and concepts. He takes care to highlight the delicate interchange of ideas in Sinology, such as the penetration of the institutionalization approach and functionalism into the Chinese IR community. After surveying various approaches, Ding concludes that Chinese foreign policy has one overriding concern — to manage domestic issues without being bogged down by regional and international entanglements. In Ding's view, China accepts the concepts of liberal institutionalization and the constructivism, especially interdependence, rules and norms to integrate itself into the world architecture.

In the next chapter, Seethi argues that the structural conditions necessary for India (and to some extent China) to emerge as the world's economic powerhouses are apparently not guaranteed. Instead of conceptualizing the rise of these two Asian powers as preordained, they could serve instead as models that are adaptable to contemporary global challenges. Rather than focusing on competition and rivalry, Seethi also sees similarities between them with great potential for exchanges and mutual sharing of ideas and developmental experiences.

Next, Morada argues against conceptualizing the ascendancy of China and India solely as a zero-sum game or balance of power rivalry. He pleads for an ASEAN not driven by the "realist" competitive balance of power which might determine or constrain its ability to engage these emerging powers to play a more positive role, and for them to become responsible stakeholders in the region. The commonalities that the two rising powers have with ASEAN states, in his view, are just as important as the differences.

In the following chapter, Saravanamuttu adopts a complex internal perspective, peering into Malaysia's racial relations and its conceptualization of Chinese and Indian minorities as well as their impact on Malaysia's relations with China and India. Malaysia negotiates its foreign relations and other externalities delicately, taking into account complexities of its multiracial internal makeup under the rubric of Malay political dominance.

Koide in the next chapter paints an anxious picture when discussing Japan's coping mechanisms with the rising China and India. He seems to differentiate the two: with the impact of China's rise felt much more keenly in Japan while India's rise still remains in the realm of perception and projection. Koide also highlights potential roles that Japan can possibly play in the post-Pax Americana global order: such as a strategic balancer between the two regional giants or an "environmental" great power.

Besides empirical, historical and geopolitical comparative studies, this edited book also looks at foreign policy themes like pragmatism and strategic thinking. Lim in the following chapter focuses on the thoughts of Michael Leifer, Kishore Mabhubani and Tommy Koh (three Singapore-centric analysts with their backgrounds straddling diplomacy and academia) on the rise of China and India. Through his analysis and portrayal of Singapore's foreign policy, one can detect the adroitness, pragmatic and strategic nature of Singapore's relations with rising powers and understand why such a small city-state has survived and prospered in an unpredictable environment.

Pragmatism is similarly examined by Prapat in the next chapter who argues that Thailand has a strategic culture acutely and skillfully attuned to shifting balances of power. Indeed, Thailand and Japan are the only two Asian countries not colonized by the West. According to Prapat, if Thailand were to adhere to this pragmatism of adapting and harnessing emerging configurations of power, the nation should not encounter serious problems but will even benefit from the rise of China and India.

The Future of India and China's Rise

That China and India are ascending in the next few decades has become a mainstream view today. However, the fate of nations is unpredictable even when things may appear to be rather rosy now. There is a saying: "Sometimes just one inch ahead is darkness". Simply put, while we may draw on the lessons of history, the future is often unpredictable. While there is much to be optimistic about the future of India and China today, many imponderables remain for them and other nations too. Conceivably, there are at least three challenges for India and China.

First, rising powers are often viewed with suspicions by other great powers which have benefited from the status quo and the rules of the game in the international political economy which they have shaped for their own interests. While the US remains the sole superpower today, it is mired in the battlefields of Iraq and Afghanistan and staring at a global finance crisis of its own making — triggered by its toxic sub-prime mortgages. This crisis has also become a contagion to global financial markets where trillions of dollars have been wiped out. While American military power and technology remains unrivaled today, economic and cultural power are much more diffused in the world. How will the US superpower deal with the rise of India and China in the decades ahead? Will the US seek to maintain its global hegemony and prevent the two Asian giants from moving up the global pecking order? Will their relationship be characterized more by competition and tension than cooperation?

Second, can India and China harmonize their relations with their smaller neighbors? Pakistan, Nepal, Sri Lanka and Bangladesh are often weary of the Indian giant next door. However, Pakistan has fought three wars with India and is now a nuclear power in its own right. Moreover, Pakistan is politically unstable and is ungovernable in the areas bordering Afghanistan much to the worry of India. Relations between China and its neighbors appear cordial with the exception of Japan which has yet to resolve its "burden of history". While the Southeast Asian countries welcome the peaceful rise of China, there are also whispers in this region asking: "China might well be peaceful when it is rising. But will China remain peaceful *after* it has risen?" In addition, territorial disputes remain between China and Vietnam, Malaysia, the Philippines and Brunei over the Spratly islands in the South China Sea. The onus is, therefore, on the two Asian giants to be considerate to the sensitivities of their smaller neighbors which will jealously safeguard their sovereignty even against larger powers.

Third, is the issue of good governance for India and China. Will both countries have good political leadership in the years ahead? Despite, the robust and time tested nature of Indian democracy, can it provide enough safety valves to accommodate its citizens including the disaffected from armed insurgency? In the case of China, can political reforms keep pace with economic development to allow its citizens more meaningful participation in policymaking? Will the Chinese leadership have the wisdom to address the desire for greater autonomy and identity among some of its ethnic minorities?

These are imponderable questions and only time can tell whether India and China can live up to the high expectations among many that they will be rising for decades to come. If both giants were to become the leading actors in the New Asian Drama and help to transform the region from the "poverty of nations" to the "wealth of nations", then their rise will not only benefit themselves but possibly spearhead a new Asian Renaissance.

Chapter 2

The Rise of China: Conflict or Harmony in East Asia?

Ding Dou

The traditional pattern of Asian structure is undergoing fundamental changes, and a new regional order is under way. Indeed, the rise of China is the primary cause for an evolving regional order. How can we understand the rise of China and its implications to the evolving Asian architecture? The Western traditional international relation studies have three popular approaches: realism, liberal institutionalization and constructivism. This chapter will adopt a combination of all three paradigms because no single approach is sufficient to explain the complex change in East Asia. My central argument is that the balance of power, economic interdependency and the forging of a common identity will have profound implications for China's rise and its impact on the region. But ultimately, the future of China lies in the uncertain development *within* China. But if the Chinese leadership can successfully address the country's domestic problems within the next two decades, China is likely to emerge as a contended power which can contribute to the peace, prosperity and harmony of East Asia.

The Realist Approach

The realism approach uses the concept of power shift to understand the rise of China, firmly emphasizing the potential dangers of China's rise. Since the dynamic rise of China as a regional or even a global economic and political player seems inevitable, the actual issue to deal with is whether and to what extent it is a peaceful shift or is it a conflictual transition. From the viewpoint of realism, the rise of China poses major challenge to the U.S.-dominated unipolar world. More specifically, Beijing would inevitably challenge Washington's hegemony in East Asia. For example, Robert Kagan argued that China aims "in the near term, to replace the United States as the dominant power in East Asia and in the long term to challenge America's position as the dominant power in the world".[3]

The realists find its deep roots in historical analysis on the rise and fall of great powers in Western history. The influential book *"The Rise and Fall of the Great Powers"* written by Paul Kennedy has gained many admirers and adherents including scholars and policy advisers in China.[4] According to the ethos of realism, the rise of China would pose a security dilemma for the U.S. and Asia. In response, how do you deal with a rising power which may challenge the status quo? Conceivably, some of Asian countries may not bandwagon, or align themselves with China but may deliberately hedge against the potential of China's dominance in Asia, and adopt balancing measures between China and the U.S.

China faces a security dilemma too. From the foundation of the People's Republic of China in 1949 till the early 1980s, the ideological orthodoxy was Marxist–Leninist–Maoism. According to this Marxist framework, world history is driven by class struggle and that inevitable competition among great powers would lead to war. While Marxism has waned in the post-Mao era, many Chinese leaders in their youth have been socialized and imbued with Marxist notions such as hegemony, imperialism, exploitation, struggle, conflict, and the correlation of forces. They are cognizant, therefore, that other powers, great and small alike, may view the rise of China not with rosy lenses but a potential threat. Simply put, the leadership generation schooled in Marxism and Maoism in China is sensitive to the notion and reality of power and conflict. In a sense, this

---

[3] Robert Kagan, What China Knows that We Don't, *The Weekly Standard*, 20 January 1997.

[4] This book was a best seller in the late 1980s in China. Three Chinese editions were published by three different Chinese publishers at that time.

residual Marxist–Maoist legacy of viewing international relations as conflict and struggle is compatible to Western international relations theory of realism. However, it does not mean China would seek to scramble to become a full-fledged challenger to the world order. On the contrary, China has learnt from history that challengers to the prevailing order can end up defeated like Germany in World War I, Germany and Japan in World War II, or suffer implosion like the Soviet Union at the end of the Cold War. As a result, China is careful not to act as a challenger but to seek to be a beneficiary of a US-led world order. In the mid-1990s, and in domestic China, there was a heated debate[5] on what kind of actor China should play in the world, and consequently, the abovementioned consensus was reached. I believe Chinese leadership accepted or was at least influenced by this widespread consensus, and adopted it in Chinese diplomatic practice.

There are many Western scholars and policy advisers who believe in the realist prism. According to the realism approach, China's rise would inevitably lead to an armed conflict with the U.S. in the future.[6] However, this realist logic is too fatalistic. Apparently, the Western realist assumption that China is a potential problem and must be dealt with either by the softer approach of engagement or the tougher strategy of containment. Engagement may emphasize diplomatic pressure while containment entails a system of military alliances against China. The danger of such realist assumptions to contain China's rise might well lead to a Sino–U.S. conflict and an unstable Asia.

Does the rise of China necessarily mean the relative decline of the U.S.? Does the resultant power shift in East Asia mean military confrontation between China and its rivals? With the ascendance of China, will the Asian regional order evolve into a Sino-centric system? I argue that history does not necessarily repeat itself and it is highly unlikely that an Asian hierarchy with the Middle Kingdom at its core will be reinstated. The world has changed too radically for such a Sino-centric

---

[5] The influential Chinese journal *Strategy and Management*, which has a military background, sponsored the debate in the mid-1990s.

[6] In the West, there are many books and articles predicting the Sino-US military conflict in the future. However, the hypothesis of a China threat is highly debatable.

system to be reestablished. Our new era can be characterized by increasing globalization, regionalism and economic interdependence, and China too is embracing these trends to its own advantage.[7]

In the post-Mao Era, Chinese leaders, scholars and policy advisers have embraced paramount leader Deng Xiaoping's dictum that China should strategically adopt a low profile in international relations and bide its time while it modernizes and strengthens itself. Therefore, they believe that the best approach to the security dilemma of China's rise is that the country should not become a challenger to the U.S. hegemon in the foreseeable future.

From the historical perspective, some Chinese scholars find there are precedents to the peaceful rise of China. The historical "tributary system"[8] (approximately the fifth through eighteenth centuries) centered around China, with the distinguished feature of the peaceful and mutually beneficial relationship between the hegemonic China and its periphery territories. It implies now that neighbors of China should remain calm about the dynamic rise of China. Apparently, the philosophy behind this argument is that history will repeat itself.

The Institutionalization Approach

An alternative approach to understanding the rise of China is the approach of liberal institutionalization. From the viewpoints of liberal institutionalists, the rise of China looks different.

This approach is inspired by the new era of globalization, which is characterized by global interdependence. The positive gains from trans-border trade, investment, communication and migration, and common problems like climate change, provide incentives for erstwhile rivals to seek mutual benefit. The basic logic of realism is the law of jungle or an intrinsically zero-sum Hobbesian struggle. In contrast, the basic

---

[7] See, for example, Robert Sutter, *China's Rise in Asia: Promises and Perils* (Lanham, MD.: Rowman and Littlefield, 2005).

[8] For understanding the tribute system, see John K. Fairbank, *The Chinese World Order: Traditional Chinese Foreign Relations* (Cambridge Mass.: Harvard University Press, 1968).

assumption of the institutionalization approach is a co-operative win–win or a positive sum game for all players. Inasmuch as the ratio of benefits/costs has changed very much (with both the costs of disruptive behavior and the benefits of cooperative behavior going up dramatically) the cooperative behavior becomes the rational option. Thus any rational country including China would more likely choose cooperation and coordination among states.

As a general reflection on global interdependence, there is an expanding network of international organizations and regimes based on common rules and norms. The concept of institution consists basically of the regime and the rules of the game. According to the institutionalization approach, it is important to integrate China into a wide range of institutions. If China becomes an active participant multinational organizations, China's aspirations for disruptive behavior would be constrained. A key reason why Hitler's Germany and imperial Japan challenged the prevailing world order was the reluctance and refusal of the status quo great powers (which benefited from the preexisting global regime and norms) to accept and accomodate the emerging powers.

Multinational institutions are considered the backbone of the world order. Current Western scholars are confident about the robustness, flexibility and openness of the ongoing world order. John Ikenberry gave his evaluation about it in *Foreign Affairs*: "The rise of China does not have to trigger a wrenching hegemonic transition. The U.S.–Chinese power transition can be very different from those of the past because China faces an international order that is fundamentally different from those that past rising states confronted. ......Today's Western order, in short, is hard to overturn and easy to join. ......Today, China can gain full access to and thrive within this system. And if it does, China will rise, but the Western order — if managed properly — will live on".[9] Indeed, since the end of World War II until now, the Western order has succeeded in integrating Japan, West Germany and the former Soviet Union into the world order.

The institutionalization approach looks exciting and encouraging to some Asian countries, which remain somewhat unsure about the

---

[9] John Ikenberry, The Rise of China and the Future of the West, *Foreign Affairs*, January/February, 2008.

orientation of the rise of China. Since the end of the Cold War, and with the accelerating globalization, multilateralism in Asia has increased rapidly, and a number of institutions have developed in tandem. It is likely that an Asian regional community with a series of common multinational institutions and shared norms will emerge. The reinforcement of ASEAN is a good illustration.

Since early 1990s in China, the institutionalization approach has begun to influence Chinese scholars and policy advisers and is being adopted in university courses. Although the open-up policy in China since the late 1970s kicked off its long process of integrating itself into the world economic order, it is since the mid-1990s that China changed its long-term suspicion of multinational architecture which could limit its sovereignty, and then embraced the world order increasingly and proactively. Now China is a member of more than 130 international and intergovernmental organizations, and its compliance behavior is evaluated well.[10]

As an unprecedented step, China joined the ASEAN's Treaty of Amity and Cooperation in the year 2003, becoming the first non-ASEAN state to do so. It means that China would be compliant to the principles of the ASEAN 1967 charter. In the same year, China signed Declaration on Conduct in the South China Sea, setting up common norms for both China and ASEAN in coping with bilateral controversies. Another attempt was to establish the famous "ASEAN plus three (China, Japan and South Korea)", which updates itself every year.

In some sense, the primary concern for Chinese diplomacy since the mid-1990s has been "how to integrate itself into the network of the multilateral institutions". However, China is aware that doing so would mean recognizing and respecting the dominant position of U.S. in Asian region. Although this was not publicly stated, China did so in practice. Until now, China's integration into the world seems to be successful. Moreover, the Chinese leadership appears to appreciate the current multilateral rules and regimes because their nation has prospered by harnessing these rules and regimes.

---

[10] Chan, G, *China's Compliance in Global Affairs*, p. 70. (New Jersey and London: World Scientific, 2006.)

The Constructivism Approach

The main concept of the constructivism approach is identity construction. The constructivists share the concepts of the institutionalization approach, such as rules and norms, and extend it into the internalization of the behaviorial norms by the individual actors. A key concept of this paradigm is socialisation which emphasizes the process of identity construction. In this regard, China's identity has been transformed from an aggrieved Maoist revolutionary state to a developmental state and a good global citizen which abides by and benefits from the norms and rules of international society.

China has embraced the world order proactively and appears to be increasingly a status quo power. However, the concern is regarding the motives behind China doing so. In short, the key question is "whether the rise of China is the rise of a potential friend or a potential enemy".[11] Apparently, the constructivism approach tries to address this question of identity: friend or foe? Some Chinese scholars agree with it, arguing that "the main variable enabling a peaceful transition was the interaction between the two countries which resulted in a change in their mutual recognition of identities".[12]

How does China perceive itself? China today faces the tension of "dual identities".

On the one hand, China regards itself as a victim of the brutal Western aggression in modern history. This historical memory of pain and humiliation leaves an indelible mark on China's perception towards the outside world and itself. The primary dream of most Chinese, including the scholars and policy advisers, is to realize the great revival and rejuvenation of the Chinese nation.[13] During the opening

---

[11] A typical attempt by a Chinese scholar using constructivism to analyze Sino-American relationship, is the following book. Wang Jianwei: *Limited Adversaries: Post-Cold War Sino-American Mutual Images* (New York: Oxford University Press, 2000).

[12] Feng Yongping, The Peaceful Transition of Power from the UK to the US, *The Chinese Journal of International Politics*, 1(1), 83–108, 2006.

[13] The great rejuvenation of Chinese nation is written into the formal documents of China's Communist Party since the late 1990s.

ceremony of the 2008 Beijing Olympics, the idea of projecting Chinese rejuvenation to the world was evident. It should be noted, however, that nationalism, or its variant "narrow" nationalism, has always intertwined with the dream of realizing China's revival.

On the other hand, China is striving to project itself as a responsible member of the world order. In light of the constructivism approach, China is now being socialized into a wide array of norms and rules, and is willing to embrace the prevailing norms and rules. Consequently, we can say that China is now gearing itself towards a global identity based on norms first established by Western statecraft.

To what extent can China balance its pursuit of national interests and its compliance to international norms? When the world expects to constructively engage China, China may constructively engage the world, especially the neighboring Asian countries. For example, China has joined various multilateral regimes with ASEAN, Southeast Asian states endorse more firmly the one-China policy, which is regarded as one of the core national interests of China. In some sense, it implies that ASEAN countries are socialized to the norm that Taiwan is an indispensable part of China. However, none of these paradigms can sufficiently and holistically explain China's international relations. I argue that future of China in the world really lies within the country itself: cumulative change in China's domestic, social, economic and political system will impact on its relations with the world.

Uncertain Development of China

We find that all the three approaches provide insights to the rise of China and its impact on Asia. However, none of these can sufficiently and holistically explain China's international relations.[14]

The most uncertain factor for the rise of China comes exactly from China itself. The rise of China is greatly supported by its economic power. However, the sustainability of Chinese economic growth remains

---

[14] Guillaume Gaulier, Francoise Lemoine, and Deniz Unal-Kesenci, China's Emergence and the Reorganization of Trade Flows in Asia, *China Economic Review*, 18, 209–243, 2007.

questionable, because China's growth is at the expense of the low-cost labor and environmental deterioration. In short, Chinese economy lacks core competitiveness. With the peaking of a young labor force and the increasing requirement of its environmental protection, the potential difficulties inside the Chinese economy would surface. In addition to the economy, China has faced many social distresses, for example, the contradiction between the poor and the rich, between the city and the countryside, between the coastal region and the hinterland etc.

In 2007, Susan Shirk wrote a book *"China: Fragile Power"*.[15] Foreigners commented on the title as "Fragile? China doesn't seem fragile", while the Chinese said, "superpower? China isn't a superpower". In 2007, *Newsweek* published an article *"The Rise of a Fierce Yet Fragile Superpower"*, which caused a stir amongst many Chinese intellectuals.

Conclusion

While China is not as fragile and unstable as some pundits claim it to be, it is undeniable that governing and modernizing a country of 1.3 billion people is no mean feat. While critics may question the motives and ambitions of Chinese leaders for their nation's rise, the truth of the matter is that the leadership is preoccupied with solving a myriad of domestic problems rather than dreaming of external aggrandizement and challenging international norms and power structures. The post-Mao Chinese leadership has accepted the norms and institutions of the global order rather than to challege let alone overthrow it. If the leadership can address its manifold domestic problems leading to a better life for most of its people over the next two decades, one can expect China to become a rising but satisfied power not bent on ill will towards its Asian neighbors and other external powers. Rather than a rising and bitter challenger leading to conflict and convulsion in the region, China might well turn out to be a contended stabilizer for a "harmonious" East Asia underpinned by economic interdependency, cultural and diplomatic exchanges and growing regionalism.

---

[15] Susan Shirk, *China: Fragile Power* (Oxford, New York: Oxford University Press, 2007).

Chapter 3

Emerging India and China: Potentials and Constraints

K. M. Seethi

The debates on the 'rise' of India and China have been underway for more than a decade, particularly since the 'Second Generation' reforms launched by the international financial institutions in the late 1990s. There are high-profile projections that India and China are poised to become the most important economic powerhouses in the world within a few decades. Many argue that India has tremendous potential to emerge as the third largest economy in the world in purchasing power parity (PPP) terms by 2020, next only to the United States and China.[16] Similarly, the 'rise' of China has been viewed from the perspective of its 'fastest growing economy' and "fastest growing military budget."[17] Thus, with a combined population of 2.5 billion (which is about 40 percent of the world's population) and amazing

---

[16] See Subhash Vohra, "China and India are Rising Economic Powers," *News VoA.com* April 9, 2007. Available at http://www.voanews.com. Also see Charan Wadhva, "India 2020: Comparative Positioning of India and China," in *Rising Powers: Event Report Abstract of Presentation* (London: Foreign Policy Centre, 2005).

[17] Judith F. Kornberg and John R. Faust, *China in World Politics: Polices, Processes, Prospects*, p. 51 (London: Lynne, Rienner, 2005). Also see Nicholas D. Kristof, "The Rise of China," *Foreign Affairs* 72, No.5, November–December (1993), 59–74.

growth rates, India and China are purported to play significant roles in international relations.

The aim of this chapter is to contest these projections as the structural conditions necessary for India (and to some extent China) to emerge as the world's economic powerhouses are apparently not well guaranteed. However, I would argue that notwithstanding all limitations, both India and China could very well set a model of partnership that can adequately meet the challenges from the global arena. This necessarily calls for a rethinking about their respective roles in domestic, regional and international settings. Leaving aside the old mindsets and stereotypical power projections, emanating from the 1962 war, the two countries should be able to pool their vital resources and work together in a more pragmatic manner in a world increasingly dictated by the ascendency of capital and perceptions of strength. While being apprehensive about the mainstream prognosis of the 'rise' of India and China, this chapter also keeps in perspective the structural shift in international relations and the emerging challenges from global economy.

India and China: Development Trajectories

India and China as 'rising great powers' have been viewed with uncritical celebration as well as concern in many of the contemporary political and economic debates.[18] Scholars argue that India and China have already attracted the attention of the world not just because of the size of the population and its 'impressive economic growth' brought about by economic reforms. The heralding of the new 'Asian century' has also been foretold with respect to the current 'success stories' of the two economies that are claimed to have taken the best advantage of globalisation with

---

[18] Kristof, 59–74. Also see Alastair Iain Johnston and Robert S. Ross (eds.), *Engaging China: The Management of an Emerging Power* (London and New York: Routledge, 1999); David S. G. Goodman and Gerald Segal (eds.), *China Rising: Nationalism and Interdependence* (London and New York: Routledge, 1997); George Perkovich, Is India a Major Power, The *Washington Quarterly* 27, No. 1, Winter (2003–04): 129–144.

'high' achievements. The valorisation of China is gaining momentum in India too, in the form of a 'longing eastern gaze.'[19]

The high growth rates of India and China are most frequently used to reinforce the economic policy of choice. Many would content that the high achievements of India and China are attributed to the economic reforms and openness to foreign trade and investment. Others, while being sceptical about India, underscore the success story of land reforms in China during the Mao period and argue that Communist China's egalitarian policies had created the essential conditions for all subsequent changes. As Samir Amin says, the differences between the Indian model and that of China "account for the visible differences in their results." The growth in China has been accompanied by a significant improvement in the people's standard of living. But the experience of India has been different "where growth exclusively benefitted the new middle classes" who constitute the minority "although in a thirty year period they expanded from 5 to 15 percent of the overall population of the country."[20]

Notwithstanding the differences in the structure and developmental trajectories, the economies of India and China are generally seen as somewhat similar from the angle of economic growth. In fact, the vast differences in the developmental trajectories make such similarities very superficial. Differences could be perceptible in the very nature and evolution of the economies, as well as in the systemic conditions within which policies have been formulated and implemented. India, until 1991, sustained a 'mixed economy' with the aim of promoting the capitalist path of development, and the postcolonial economic policies of India were intended to stimulate demand, typical of a capitalist economy, without undermining the welfare-developmental role of the state. China, on the other hand, maintained a command economy with a lot of self-regulating mechanisms. During the period of liberalisation, particularly after 1990s, there was, still, state control over macroeconomic

---

[19] Jayati Ghosh, "China and India: The Big Differences," August 24(2005). Available at http://www.macroscan.org/cur/aug05/cur240805China_India.htm.
[20] Samir Amin, "India, a Great Power," *Monthly Review*, 56(9), February (2005), 6–7.

processes which was different from conventional capitalist macroeconomic policy. For instance, even in 2004, public enterprises contributed to more than half of GDP and more than two-fifths of exports.[21] In the financial sector too, the state control has been important. The scenario in India is totally different.

The economic growth rate of China has been very high for long unlike the more moderate expansion in India. China reported a growth rate of 10.4 percent in the first half of 2008.[22] The economy registered an average annual growth rate of 9.8 percent for the last 25 years, while India's economy has grown at around 5–6 percent per year over the same period. As the process of economic liberalisation advanced in India, economic growth began to show some improvement — from an average of 3.7 percent in the 1950s and 1960s to a level of 6 percent in the 1990s and reached 9 percent recently.[23]

The higher growth in China is reported to have occurred because of much higher rate of investment in China. The investment rate in China (as share of GDP) has swung between 35 and 44 percent over the past 25 years, compared to 20 to 26 percent in India. Within this, there is the critical role of infrastructure investment, which has averaged at 19 percent of GDP in China compared to 2 percent in India over the 1990s.[24] Many argue that China can afford to have such a high investment rate because it has, over years, attracted so much foreign direct investment (FDI), and is the second largest recipient of FDI in the world.[25]

---

[21] Ghosh (2005).

[22] World Trade Organization, *International trade and tariff data, China* (Geneva: WTO, 2008). Available at http://stat.wto.org/CountryProfile/WSDBCountryPFView.aspx?Language=E&Country=CN.

[23] World Trade Organization, *International trade and tariff data, India* (Geneva: WTO, 2008). Available at http://stat.wto.org/CountryProfile/WSDBCountryPFView.aspx?Language=E&Country=IN.

[24] Ghosh (2005).

[25] World Bank, *China Quarterly Update June 2008* (Washington, DC: World Bank, 2008). Available at http://www.worldbank.org/. Also see Christopher Findlay and Andrew Watson, "Economic growth and trade dependency in China," in *China Rising: Nationalism and Interdependence* ed. David S. G. Goodman and Gerald Segal, 113 (London and New York: Routledge, 1997).

The Chinese success here is again attributed to its location. The east coast of China is situated in a highly dynamic and rich neigbourhood. Countries like Japan, South Korea, Taiwan, Hong Kong and Singapore continued to provide capital for investment, markets for Chinese exports, advanced technology and expertise. South Asia is less dynamic where 40 percent of the world's poor live and, more importantly, very few transfers take place between India and its South Asian neighbours.

In India there has been a shift from agriculture to services in the share of output, with no substantial increase in manufacturing, and the structure of employment has been extremely vulnerable. India's economic transition has apparently skipped the industrialisation phase and advanced, instantly, to a services sector-led economy, which constitutes about 50 percent of GDP, compared with 25 percent five decades ago.[26] China, on the other hand, has moved from primary to manufacturing sector and doubled its share of workforce and tripled its share of output, which, given the size of the Chinese economy and population, has made China 'the workshop of the world.'[27] This change of position, according to some scholars, increased China's dependence on the rest of the world as a source of raw materials, as a source of capital and as a market for products.[28] Meanwhile, agriculture has been declining as a proportion of the economy and the competing demand for food and agricultural raw materials place great pressures on supply. Various studies say that the shrinking arable land and the surging population point to the fact that China has no comparative advantage in agricultural production.[29] UNDP's China Human Development Report 2005 (prepared mostly by Chinese economists) says that the spectacular achievements of China have been accompanied by growing inequalities of income and

---

[26] Jennifer Asuncion-Mund, *India Rising: A Medium-term Perspective: India Special* (Frankfurt: Deutsche Bank Research, 2005). Available at www.dbresearch.com

[27] Ghosh (2005).

[28] Findlay and Watson (1997), pp. 108–109.

[29] Kym Anderson, *Changing Comparative Advantages in China: Effects on Food, Feed and Fibre markets* (Paris: OECD Development Studies, 1990).

wealth distribution. The Report focused on the issue of inequality in economic and human development indicators. It also points to the widening inequality within rural and urban areas based on a survey conducted a few years ago.[30] Yet, China has been quite successful in tackling poverty. Official statistics indicate that only 4 percent of the population now lives under the poverty line (unofficial sources put the figure 12 percent). The success story of China is attributed to the redistribution of wealth and the basic needs provision available till the late 1970s.

Emerging India: Challenges

India's role in the emerging international system is based not on its military or economic power status, as many would have us believe, but on its ability to build new coalitions of bargain in a world of 'complex interdependence.'[31] During the cold war period, India had been very active in mobilising Third World countries by building coalitions in international relations through non-aligned movement(NAM), Commonwealth, Group of 77, United Nations Conference on Trade and Development (UNCTAD), etc.[32] In fact, India's 'strategic isolation' (euphemism for non-alignment) and proactive policy evolved and operated within the structural constraints of the domestic and international system. The Bandung spirit provided the necessary dynamism for its self-assertion in a global system dominated by two antagonistic power blocs and the structures of the world economy. However, India never sought to delink itself from world capitalism — as its economy had already been

---

[30] C.P. Chandrasekhar and Jayati Ghosh, "Rising Inequality in China," *The Hindu*, January 3, 2006.

[31] See Robert O. Keohane and Joseph S. Nye Jr, *Power and Interdependence* (Boston: Little, Brown and Company, 1977); Robert O. Keohane, and Joseph S. Nye, Jr., "Power and Interdependence in the information age," *Foreign Affairs*, September–October (1998), pp. 81–95.

[32] K.M. Seethi and Vijayan P., "Political Economy of India's Third World Policy," in *Engaging with the World: Critical Reflections on India's Foreign Policy*, Rajen Harshe and K.M. Seethi (eds.), pp. 47–69 (New Delhi: Orient Longman, 2005).

integrated into the world economy through a global system of appropriation during colonialism[33] — but displayed greater maneuverability within the limitations imposed by the circumstances of the world situation. The Nehru government, thus, used foreign policy as a powerful instrument to bargain with the power blocs. As such the role of India was very significant in mobilising countries in the developing world, particularly for the democratisation of the prevailing international political and economic order.

Over years, India, along with other developing countries, understood the imperative to position development issues ahead of political issues and to make the best use of coalitions in various international fora. The change of emphasis from cold war issues (along an East-West axis) towards rich-poor issues (along a North-South axis) was symbolic both of changes in the world system and the increase in the influence of the developing world.[34] The Declaration on the establishment of the New International Economic Order (NIEO) adopted by the UN General Assembly in 1974 was an earnest attempt in this direction.[35] The agenda of NIEO put in place the redistribution of the world's wealth and economic resources, and the restructuring of the international economic system and its institutions — to guarantee that the vital interests of developing countries were protected. It was to be based on the principles of equity, sovereign equality, interdependence, common interest and cooperation among all states.

However, the debates on the issues raised though NIEO did not last long as many of the industrialised nations began to face acute crisis characterised by unparalleled stagnation coupled with worsening inflation(stagflation) resulting in an unprecedented fall in agricultural and

---

[33] Immanuel Wallerstein, "Incorporation of Indian subcontinent into capitalist world economy," *Economic and Political Weekly*, XXI, No. 4, January 25, 1986, pp. 28–39.

[34] Timothy M. Shaw, "The Non-Aligned Movement and the New International Economic Order," in *Transforming the World Economy?* Herb Addo, (ed.), p. 142 (Tokyo: United Nations Publications, 1999).

[35] United Nations, General Assembly, *Declaration of the Establishment of a New International Economic Order, 2229th Plenary Meeting, 1 May* (New York: UN, 1974).

industrial production, and a rise in unemployment and prices. The US-led industrialised countries sought to address the situation by transferring the burden of this mounting crisis to the shoulders of African-Asian-Latin American countries, which resulted in a new cycle of global appropriation by international capital using the multilateral institutions like IMF, World Bank and GATT.[36] The inevitable consequence of this transfer of burden was the deepening economic crisis in many countries, most importantly in India.

Thus, in the 1980s, India took decisions which altered the very paradigm of development, reoriented economic agenda and prepared the ground for a far-reaching transition. The irreversible balance of payment situation in the late 1980s created the necessary conditions for structural adjustments stipulated by the IMF.[37] Thus, much before the tectonic shift in world politics in 1991, the Indian economy experienced a deepening integration with world economy and international capital, and it became more vulnerable to international economic fluctuations over which it could exercise no control whatsoever.[38]

The economic reforms launched in 1991[39] and the subsequent import-export policies were in tune with the trade-liberalisation prescriptions of the IMF-World Bank combine. Later, with the emergence of the World Trade Organisation (WTO), as a global trade mechanism, India's obligations to international capital have become so deep that they have made the social welfare/security agenda of the Indian state completely obsolete. The neoliberal economic reforms, thus, brought about a paradigm shift in the very philosophy of development which made the Indian economy more susceptible to the pressures of the IMF-World Bank-WTO triad, on the one hand, and the advanced capitalist countries, on the other. At the domestic level, the 'exclusive beneficiaries'

---

[36] Susan George, *A Fate Worse than Debt: The World Financial Crisis and the Poor* (New York: Grove Weidenfeld, 1990).

[37] Bimal Jalan, *India's Economic Crisis — The Way Ahead* (New Delhi: Oxford University Press, 1991).

[38] Seethi and Vijayan, pp. 47–60.

[39] India, Ministry of Finance, *Economic Survey 1991–92* (New Delhi: Ministry of Finance, 1992).

of the neoliberal regime were the big industrialists (monopoly houses), capitalist farmers and rural landlords, the urban middle class, bureaucrats, and professional elites who constituted the social base for the economic liberalisation.[40] These 'exclusive beneficiaries' of the neoliberal reforms are, however, to face challenges "under the effect, among others, of the end of the upward social mobility of the lower middle classes who are threatened with loss of job security and impoverishment, if not outright poverty."[41] Various studies noted that the poverty rate in India, which was about 50 percent of the population in the early years of independence, reached 26–34 percent (depending on the methodology of accounting) today. Thus, the number of people living below the poverty line in India is about 350 million which is apparently the combined population of several European countries. According to World Bank economists, India's economic growth, which has mainly been pushed by services, has not significantly helped reduce poverty since the majority of India's poor still live in rural villages that depend on agriculture, which lags behind the overall level of economic growth.[42]

Even social development indicators offer a dismal picture of India. *The Human Development Report 2007–08* recorded India's rank as 128. This low rank put India in the bottom 50 of the 177 nations that the UNDP Human Development Report examined. Its present Human Poverty Index (HDI) of 0.619 is above the regional average of 0.611 for South Asia but far below 0.691 for developing countries. India as a high growth economy, with per capita incomes rising at an average of 4–5 percent since the mid-90s, is believed to have created enormous opportunities for accelerated human development. But the growth has not produced poverty reduction and improvement in nutrition. About 500 million

---

[40] Prabhat Patnaik, "International Capital and National Economic Policy: A Critique of India's Economic Reforms," *Economic and Political Weekly*, 29(12), 1994, 683–90.

[41] Amin, 11.

[42] See Martin Ravallion and Gaurav Datt, "Why Has Economic Growth Been More Pro-Poor in Some States of India than Others," *Journal of Development Economics*, 68, (2002), 381–444. http://poverty.worldbank.org/files/13995_JDE2002.pdf)

people in the country do not have access to modern electricity. Besides India stands at 62 in the Human Poverty Index (HPI) among the 108 developing countries. HPI represents people living below a $1 per day earning.[43] Various estimates suggest that 77 percent of India's working population lives on less than Rs.20 per day, which is about half a US dollar a day.

The robust economic growth of India (at an average of 8.8 percent) during the last five years, reaching 9 percent last year, is no guarantee of stability because this has been accompanied by surging inflation touching a record of 12.44 percent in the first week of August 2008. *The Economic Outlook for 2008–09* presented by the Prime Minister's Economic Advisory Council (EAC) now forecasts that the GDP growth rate of India would be falling to 7.7 percent for the next few months and the inflation may cross 13 percent alongside this. It also pointed out that the agricultural growth rate is to drop sharply from 4.5 percent in 2007–08 to a mere 2 percent this year. Non-farm sector GDP is also projected to slow down (8.9 percent compared to 10 percent last year). The Indian economy, by and large, faces great supply constraints, particularly in physical and social infrastructure.[44]

Scholars may argue that the world economy as a whole is facing this slow down consequent upon the food and fuel inflation and the financial sector crisis. But the effects of such global crisis on particular countries are vastly different and the capacity to withstand such pressures also varies from country to country. India and China are classical examples. India has already shown its volatility vis-à-vis the global economy. Though China has much greater resilience in coping with the global crisis, it too will have to share the burden in the long run given the nature of its trade pattern. It also has another dimension — whatever fluctuations and instability in China's trading pattern could have negative

---

[43] See United Nations Development Programme, *Human Development Report 2007–08, Fighting Climate Change: Human Solidarity in a Divided World* (New York: UNDP, 2008).

[44] India, Prime Minister's Office, *Economic Outlook for 2008/09* (New Delhi: Economic Advisory Council to the Prime Minister of India, 2008). Available at http://www.pmindia.nic.in/eac_report_08.pdf

impacts on its trading partners, particularly those countries having high stakes in China trade.[45] However, in spite of all odds, China's share in world trade has been showing an upward trend during the last three decades. For example, in 1978, China accounted for less than 1 percent of global trade, while in 2007, the figure rose to about 8 percent, with an average annual import growth of 16.7 percent. China has grown into the third largest import market in the world and the largest in Asia.[46]

On the other side, the share of India's merchandise exports in world trade was a meager 0.67 percent during the year 2000, even after a decade of economic reform.[47] According to WTO, India's share in total world trade, which includes trade in both merchandise and services sector increased from 1.1 percent in 2004 — i.e., the initial year of the five-year foreign trade policy (2004–09) to 1.5 percent in 2006.[48] It is hoped that the country's share in global merchandise trade might increase from 1.2 percent in 2006 to 1.5 percent in 2009.[49] Still India's performance is far from satisfactory.

There are obvious domestic constraints to India's emergence as a major power. These are the challenges one can see in the social and cultural spheres. While communalism, fundamentalism and terrorism continued to threaten the social fabric of Indian society, successive governments are hard-pressed to deal with the Naxalite uprisings in certain parts of the country. The role of caste is still important as an

---

[45] Findlay and Watson, 114.

[46] People's Republic of China, Ministry of Foreign Affairs, "China-US Relations in the New Century," Speech by Foreign Minister Yang Jiechi at the Luncheon Marking the Inauguration of the Kissinger Institute on China and the United States at the Wilson Center, 2008/07/30. Available at http://www.fmprc.gov.cn/eng/wjdt/zyjh/t461226.htm.

[47] India, Ministry of Commerce and Industry, "India's Share in World Trade," July 27, 2001. Available at http://commerce.nic.in/PressRelease/pressrelease_detail.asp?id=540.

[48] World Trade Organization, *International Trade and Tariff Data, India.*

[49] India, Directorate General of Commercial Intelligence and Statistics, Ministry of Commerce and Industry, *Provisional Monthly Foreign Trade data, 2008.* Available at http://www.dgciskol.nic.in/.

agency for social and political mobilisation. This often results in political uncertainty and instability in certain states like Uttar Pradesh. Quite surprisingly, even left parties have come to reckon the role of caste in electoral politics in recent times. The growth of caste, religion, and other identities, thus, continues to be a critical factor in determining India's image as a 'rising' power in the 20th century.

The above accounts of India's overall socio-economic position show that it would be premature to predict that India would be a 'beacon of hope' in the 21st century and its economy would be the world's third largest by 2020. The fact that India's position in the world trade has not grown at a faster rate than its economic growth is an indication of its dependency and the very complex paradigm of development trajectory. What lies ahead before India is therefore a world of uncertainties and trepidations.

India and China in the New 'Asian Century'

A few years ago, the Chinese leader Hu Jintao said that "China's development would be impossible without Asia, and Asia's prosperity without China."[50] This is a fact to be reckoned with by India and other countries in the Asian region. India's relations with East and Southeast Asia are already dynamic and more positive than at any time in history. This is also a region where China has high stakes. In fact, New Delhi's 'Look East policy', enunciated way back in the early 1990s, strengthened the strategic initiatives in improving ties with countries in the region. However, a key to the success of Indian diplomacy in the larger terrain of Asia-Pacific lies in finding out a new accommodative space with China. It may be noted that India-China relations have already shown considerable improvement during the last two decades. Since 1988 the two countries have been pursuing a proactive policy of strengthening economic ties and addressing sensitive areas of bilateral relations more positively, including the unsettled border dispute. What facilitated the process were the major shifts in the global economic,

---

[50] Alice D. B, "China and ASEAN: Renavigating Relations for a 21st Century Asia," *Asian Survey* 42, No. 4, July–August (2003), pp. 622–647.

political and security architecture in the early 1990s that had opened up a conducive environment for deepening the bilateral relations.

Economic relations constitute the most dynamic aspect of bilateral ties between India and China. The trade between the two has grown remarkably well over the last one decade. The bilateral trade has expanded at a 50 percent rate during the last six years and is expected to increase by a further 54 percent in the coming years. India's trade with China has doubled in the last two years. The trade target of $20 billion by 2008 was reached two years ahead of schedule. The revised target of $40 billion by 2010 is also likely to be achieved two years ahead of schedule.[51] During Prime Minister Manmohan Singh's visit to China in January 2008, it was decided to increase the trade target from $40 billion to $60 billion by 2010. It may be noted that India's trade with China is greater than that with Japan, the US, or the entire world. After similar adjustments, China's trade with India is only slightly below that with Japan, the US, or the entire world. During Manmohan Singh's visit the two countries also signed a document 'Shared Vision for the 21st Century' which reflects not only the common perceptions of India and China but also their desire to purposefully cooperate in the future and to promote global durable peace and common prosperity on the basis of Panchsheel. The most important aspect of the document is that the two sides favoured an "open and inclusive international system."[52]

However, even as trade and other transactions have surged over years, there are some sections of people within India (particularly in the defence and foreign policy establishments as well as among the political parties) who remain suspicious of China, particularly in the context of its relationship with Pakistan, India's long-term rival in South Asia. This happens whenever India needs to justify its high-profile military

---

[51] India, Ministry of External Affairs, *Annual Report 2007–2008* (New Delhi: MEA, 2008); Ralph J. Tyler "The future of India-China trade," *The Economic Times*, January 14, 2008.

[52] India, Ministry of External Affairs, "PM'S address at the India-China Economic, Trade and Investment Summit," January 14, 2008. Available at http://meaindia.nic.in/. Also see India, *Annual Report 2007–2008*.

expenditure, and it mainly comes in the form of reinforcing threat perceptions in relation to Pakistan and China. For example, when the BJP-led National Democratic Alliance (NDA) ruled India during 1998–2004, it conveniently deployed both China and Pakistan as principle security threats to rationalise its militarisation drive, both conventional and nuclear.[53] It may also be noted that the NDA government justified India's nuclear tests in 1998 pointing to the threat China posed to its national security.[54]

However, a significant change in India's perceptions and policies came when the Congress-led United Progressive Alliance (UPA), supported by the left parties, initiated steps to strengthen relations with China. A whole series of agreements signed during the last four years show that India-China relations have dramatically improved. Some analysts, on the other side, generate fears that Washington would prefer to 'contain' China by encircling it with American allies such as India.[55] One commentator even suggested that in order to woo Washington (following Pokhran-II nuclear tests), "India must challenge China because India and the West have similar strategic aims concerning containing China."[56] But China is far more realistic in dealing with India, United States and Pakistan. Beijing, in fact, desires normalisation with India without undermining its strategic engagement with Pakistan. Besides, it feels that when Sino-Indian relations improve, New Delhi will be forced to smoothen its ties with Islamabad.[57] China views its

---

[53] India, Ministry of Defence, *Annual Report 2004–05* (New Delhi: Ministry of Defence, 2005), pp. 8–13.

[54] For details, see India, Ministry of External Affairs, *Foreign Affairs Record*, 45(5), 1998; India, Ministry of Defence *Annual Report 1998–1999* (New Delhi: Ministry of Defence, 1999). Also see K.M. Seethi, "India's CTBT Policy: From 'Text' to 'Testing Times'," in *Engaging with the World: Critical Reflections on India's Foreign Policy,* Rajen Harshe and K.M. Seethi (eds).

[55] Judith F. Kornberg and John R. Faust, *China in World Politics: Polices, Processes, Prospects* (London: Lynne Rienner, 2005), p. 177.

[56] Mohan Malik J., "South Asia in China's Foreign Relations," *Pacifica Review*, 13(1), February (2001), p. 80.

[57] Jay Solomon, Charles Hutzler and Zahid Hussain, "China Steps Up Diplomatic Role," *Wall Street Journal*, December 8, 2003.

relations with the United States in a larger context of trade and investment. China and the United States are now each other's second largest trading partner. China is the third largest and the fastest growing export market for the US in the last six years. By the end of May 2008, the United States had invested over $58.1 billion in more than 55,000 projects in China, covering a wide range of sectors, including, among others, agriculture, manufacturing and financial services. China and the United States have also intensified dialogue and expanded cooperation in such fields as energy and resources, environmental protection and macro-economic policies.[58]

Given the nature of China's greater international involvement, the question facing the countries in the Asian region is not how to 'contain' China but how to meet the challenges emanating from the global economy in greater association with China. This is important from the point of view of peace and development in Asia. China's worldview now holds that developed and developing countries should "establish equal, mutually beneficial and win-win partnerships for global development and promote economic globalization towards balance, benefits for all and win-win results for all." It seeks "to build up an inclusive and orderly international financial system" and countries "should make joint efforts to increase the say and representation of developing countries in international financial institutions and improve the effectiveness of international financial system."[59]

Speaking at a meeting in Japan, Chinese President Hu Jintao said that developing countries should "work together to promote multilateralism and democracy in international relations, enhance the right of developing countries to participation and decision-making in international affairs and strive for more favorable external conditions for the growth of developing countries." He underlined the need for pushing "forward reforms in international economic, financial, trade and development regimes, uphold the legitimate rights and interests of developing

---

[58] People's Republic of China, "China–US Relations in the New Century."
[59] People's Republic of China, Ministry of Foreign Affairs, President Hu Jintao's Speech at the Meeting between the Leaders of G8 and Developing Nations, July 9 2008. Available at http://www.fmprc.gov.cn/eng/wjdt/zyjh/t455676.htm.

countries and enhance their capacity to tackle various risks and challenges, and promote balanced, coordinated and sustainable growth of the global economy."[60] China is now vigorously promoting an agenda of "balanced, coordinated and sustainable development of world economy" through South-South cooperation and North-South dialogue, an agenda that India had long held fast, but abandoned in the course of its economic reforms.

There is hardly any doubt that the financial meltdown currently sweeping across the world is the worst after the Great Depression of 1929–30. It foreshadows its most awful effect on the world economy, and the worst impact of it will be felt, sooner or later, in the developing countries. The hub of the global capital — the United States, Europe and Japan — witnessed unprecedented recession, takeovers, and state intervention. The impact of the global meltdown on the economies of the developing countries has already been felt. Those countries which have been dependent on the US, European Union and other global market are under stress as their export opportunities are considerably curtailed. For instance, the financial meltdown in the global markets has had an impact on the IT and BPO (Business Process Outsourcing) sector in India, which has targeted to achieve an export revenue of 60 billion US dollars. According to National Association of Software and Service Companies (NASSCOM), the United States is one of the largest contributors to the revenues of BPO companies, as much as 60 percent. The US financial sector, in turn, is one of the largest customers and the liquidity crunch that has hit these companies will directly cause them to start rethinking. But it says that the future hiring rate of BPOs will be far worse off. The BPO employment rate is projected to decline by 60 percent within a span of one year. Notwithstanding such high projections, experts say that the setbacks in the global economy will adversely affect India's exports, especially its exports of software and IT-enabled services, more than 60 percent of which are directed to the United States. International

---

[60] People's Republic of China, Ministry of Foreign Affairs, Remarks by Hu Jintao President of the People's Republic of China at Collective Meeting of Leaders of Five Developing Countries, Japan, July 8, 2008. Available at http://www.fmprc.gov.cn/eng/wjdt/zyjh/t455737.htm.

banks and financial institutions in the US and EU are important sources of demand for such services, and the difficulties they face will result in some curtailment of their demand. Further, the nationalization of many of these banks is likely to increase the pressure to reduce outsourcing in order to keep jobs in the developed countries. The debacle in the US would, no doubt, create a lot of uncertainties regarding the continuity of current financial services contracts and also raise doubts as to how the future contracts are signed with the US financial companies. This applies to China also.

As India and China face the future, uncertainties abound over internal and international challenges that are inextricably intertwined overlapping political boundaries. Observers mostly agree that a country's strength, particularly in the economic sense, will determine its position in the new century. An important element of this strength is internal stability based on sound management of domestic cleavages, resulting from rising inequality (within and between regions), shrinking job market, poor standard of living and social and political exclusions. Here the experiences of India and China are vastly different. Plausibly, the challenges before these nations of 2.5 billion are numerous and formidable, and they cannot be addressed without building new coalitions of bargain and negotiation in an increasingly complex interdependent world. Asia will most likely emerge as the fulcrum of this terrain of coalitions with China, Japan and India playing significant roles in setting an agenda for the future.

Chapter 4

The Rise of China and India and Its Implications for Southeast Asia: A Philippine Perspective

Noel M. Morada[61]

Introduction

The emergence of China and India as regional powers has been a subject of much speculation in Southeast Asia. Often, certain images have been used — rightly or wrongly — to portray scenarios, meanings, and consequences of China's and India's rise, based on some realist assumptions about their interest as emerging powers.

This chapter attempts to discuss some of the images associated with the growing influence of China and India in the context of Southeast Asia. It discusses issues and concerns related to their influence in the region, including the Philippines. The main argument of this chapter is that the rise of China and India should not be seen solely in the context of zero-sum game or balance of power rivalry. In particular, ASEAN

---

[61] Associate Professor of Political Science, Department of Political Science, University of the Philippines Diliman, Quezon City, and Vice Chair, Board of Directors, Institute for Strategic and Development Studies (ISDS), Inc., Quezon City, The Philippines. Paper presented at the Gandhi–Ikeda Peace Research Conference, organized by the East Asia Institute, National University of Singapore, 21 August 2008.

should not let this "realist" framework determine or constrain its ability to engage these emerging powers to play a more positive role and for them to become responsible stakeholders in the region. As ASEAN states adopt a hedging strategy in dealing with these emerging powers, it is also important not to lose sight of more fundamental human security concerns that are also shared by China and India. This does not mean, however, that the Philippines and other ASEAN states should ignore continuing tensions in their relations with China and India, especially those pertaining to traditional security issues like territorial disputes.

Imaging the Rise of China and India: Competition for Influence and Regional Power Rivalry

A number of images pertaining to the rise of China and India have been portrayed. These images essentially point to their competing economic interests and regional power rivalry. Often, China is portrayed as having the edge over India in pursuing its strategic interests in East Asia, including Southeast Asia, because the latter is a latecomer and late-bloomer in the context of globalization and regional economic integration.

Competing economic interests

China and India are competing for economic influence in Southeast Asia. This competition is manifested in terms of pushing for their respective free trade agreements with ASEAN, bilateral agreements on resource extraction, and increasing their economic influence through aid and assistance in the CLMV (Cambodia, Laos, Myanmar and Vietnam).

Beijing first proposed a free trade agreement (FTA) with ASEAN in November 2000 during the ASEAN Plus Three Summit. Subsequently, a Framework Agreement on ASEAN–China Comprehensive Economic Cooperation was signed in Phnom Penh in November 2002, which covers cooperation in goods, services, and investments, among others. In 2003, formal talks on China–ASEAN Free Trade Area (CAFTA) began, with a target implementation of 2010 for the ASEAN 6 (original members and Brunei) and 2015 for CLMV. China's motivations for proposing CAFTA include: 1) its entry into the WTO, which could be exploited by other countries to highlight the "economic threat" posed by China vis-à-vis ASEAN; 2) its direct application of China's "new security concept", which advocates a multi-polar world order and multilateralism in order to dilute American unilateralism; and 3) the promotion of East Asian integration to protect China from the negative impacts of globalization.[62]

Meanwhile, as a latecomer in engaging ASEAN,[63] India's FTA with ASEAN was not concluded until early August 2008 following three years of strenuous negotiations. The agreement will come into force in beginning 1 January 2009, or a year earlier than the CAFTA target for the ASEAN 6. While the collective FTA with ASEAN ran into difficulties, India's bilateral FTA negotiations with some ASEAN countries were smooth. Specifically, the India–Thailand Comprehensive Economic Cooperation Agreement (CECA) came into effect in 2003, while the India–Singapore CECA was implemented in August 2005.[64] Primarily, India's FTA with ASEAN was motivated by its desire to gain foothold in the large and emerging market of ASEAN. Initially, New Delhi's engagement with the countries of the region was through economic and technical assistance to new members of ASEAN and providing unilateral tariff concessions to CLMV.[65] Later, at the Third India–ASEAN Summit in Vientiane in 2004, New Delhi signed a partnership agreement with ASEAN that set the roadmap for its long-term engagement with the group. More importantly, with strong endorsement from Singapore, Indonesia, and Thailand, India became a participant in the East Asia Summit (EAS) in 2005. By having strong links with ASEAN,

---

[62] Sheng Lijun, "China–ASEAN Free Trade Area: Origins, Developments, and Strategic Motivations," ISEAS Working Paper, International Politics & Security Issues Series No. 1 (2003), pp. 6–7.

[63] India did not become a dialogue partner of ASEAN until 2002.

[64] Zhao Hong, India and China: Rivals or Partners in Southeast Asia?, *Journal of Contemporary Southeast Asia*, Vol. 29, No. 1 (April 2007), pp. 126–127.

[65] Ibid., p. 124.

India is attempting to gain access in the APEC forum and Asia-Europe Meeting (ASEM), which could give it "big power" recognition in the region.

Apart from FTAs, China and India are also involved in resource extraction competition in Southeast Asia. In Myanmar, for example, both powers are after oil and natural gas exploration. China is also known to pursue oil and hydrocarbon exploration in Cambodia[66] and is also reportedly engaged in timber trade that is often in excess of legal limits in Cambodia, Myanmar, and Indonesia.[67] Some Chinese companies are said to be involved in unregulated mining and land grabbing in Cambodia.[68] Meanwhile, India and Vietnam entered into a strategic partnership agreement in July 2007, which covers, among other things, mutual investments and joint ventures in hydrocarbon and power sectors, as well as setting up of oil refineries in Vietnam by Indian oil companies.[69]

Moreover, China and India are also competing for economic influence in Southeast Asia through sub-regional cooperation frameworks. India, for example, initiated in 2000 the "Mekong–Ganges River Cooperation Project" with five other ASEAN states (Cambodia, Laos, Myanmar, Thailand, and Vietnam). It is also a member of the BIMSTEC (Bangladesh, India, Myanmar, Sri Lanka, Thailand Economic Cooperation), which was launched in 2004. These projects apparently underscore the desire of India to enhance its links with ASEAN neighbors that share its

---

[66] David Fullbrook, China's growing influence in Cambodia, *The Asia Times Online*, 6 October 2006. Available at http://www.atimes.com/atimes/Southeast_Asia/HJ06Ae01.html. Accessed on 18 August 2008.

[67] Peter S. Goodman and Peter Finn, Corruption Stains Timber Trade, *Washington Post*, 1 April 2007, p. A01. Available at 3http://www.washingtonpost.com/wp-dyn/content/article/2007/03/31/AR2007033101287.html. Accessed on 18 August 2008.

[68] China's Growing Presence in Cambodia, *Radio Free Asia*, 5 May 2008. Available at http://www.rfa.org/english/news/cambodia/cambodia_china-05232008092653.html. Accessed on 18 August 2008.

[69] Vietnam, India issue joint declaration on strategic partnership, *VietnamNetBridge*, 7 July 2007. Available at http://english.vietnamnet.vn/politics/2007/07/715169/. Accessed on 18 August 2008.

cultural heritage, ostensibly countering China's cultural influence in Southeast Asia. New Delhi had also proposed in 2004 to undertake a railway project with ASEAN that would cut across India, Myanmar, Thailand, Laos, Cambodia, and into Hanoi in Vietnam. It is said that this project is India's response to China's "Pan-Asian Railway" project that would open a new trade corridor in the sub-Mekong region.[70] It must be noted that China's Yunnan province is member of the Greater Mekong Subregion (GMS) that groups together the five Southeast Asian Mekong states.

Regional power rivalry

Competition for power and military influence in the region is another image attributed to the rise of China and India. Indeed, as emerging military powers both may be expected in the long run to flex their muscles especially as their sustained economic development will undoubtedly enable them to improve and project their military capabilities. Myanmar is likely to remain a major arena in the region for projecting these two powers' military influence as both Beijing and New Delhi are expected to continue cultivating strong ties with the military junta in that country in exchange for access to natural resources. Meanwhile, in an effort to counter China's growing military influence in Southeast Asia (principally through military assistance and defense cooperation agreements with ASEAN countries), India's navy has conducted a number of joint military exercises with some ASEAN states (notably Singapore and Vietnam) as well as with the Japanese and South Korean navies. For their part, some ASEAN members have adopted a more benign attitude towards India even as they see it as a counterbalance vis-à-vis China, given its nuclear capability and strong presence in the Indian Ocean.[71]

It is interesting to note that it is not only ASEAN that sees the strategic importance of engaging India in the region. The United States

---

[70] Zhao Hong, Ibid., pp. 131–132.
[71] Ibid., p. 133.

and Japan also see this as an important factor in dealing with China's growing influence in Southeast Asia and East Asia at large. At the same time, however, they recognize that India still has a lot of catching up to do vis-à-vis China.

The next section of this paper examines the implications of the rise of China and India for Southeast Asia by looking into their respective "soft power" capabilities in the context of promoting human security, good governance, and human development. It will discuss the state of relations of the Philippines vis-à-vis China and India. Likewise, a discussion of potential areas of cooperation between China, India, and ASEAN in the areas of non-traditional security (NTS) issues, breaking the impasse in Myanmar, and norm building in the context of East Asia Community will also be presented.

ASEAN and the Rise of China and India: Implications for the Philippines, ASEAN, and East Asia[72]

Relations with the Philippines: China ahead of India

China's and India's relations with the Philippines are currently lop-sided in favor of the former. Much of this has to do with the fact that China has been cultivating stronger relations with ASEAN members for the past decade through what has been termed as "charm diplomacy". Geographic proximity with China, along with a sizeable presence of Chinese communities in the Philippines and other Southeast Asian countries, is also another advantage that China has over India in this part of the world.

In general, Filipinos have a positive attitude towards China's rise and, together with Japan and the United States, expect it to behave

---

[72] Parts of this section of the chapter on the Philippines and China relations were taken from the author's chapter on "The Rise of China and Regional Responses: A Philippine Perspective," in *The Rise of China and Regional Responses*, forthcoming in 2009 to be published by the National Institute of Defense Studies (NIDS), Tokyo, Japan.

responsibly as a major power. This is evident in the results of the survey conducted by the Chicago Council on Global Affairs' World Public Opinion in 2007. Specifically, the survey reported the following with regard to the perception of the Philippine public on the rise of China, as well as towards Japan and the United States:[73]

- 57% say they trust China to act responsibly in the world. That's fewer than trust Japan (67%) and far fewer than trust the US (85%).
- Majorities are confident that China, Japan and the United States will act responsibly in the world.
- Filipinos — unlike most other publics — do not believe that China's economy will catch up with the US economy.
- Only 38% of Filipinos believe that China will catch up with the US economically, while a plurality (42%) believes that the US economy will always be larger than China's.
- Most Filipinos say that it would be equally positive and negative (42%) or mostly positive (26%) if China [was] to catch up with the United States. Just 17% say it would be mostly negative.

It is clear from the above that Filipinos still have very strong affinity vis-à-vis the United States compared to China and Japan, owing perhaps to the strong cultural ties between the two countries. However, it is also significant to note that a good majority of Filipinos trusts China to act responsibly as a major power.

Meanwhile, no recent survey report on public perceptions and attitudes in the Philippines about India's rise has been produced. However, if various official statements and media reports are any indication, they generally welcome India's rise as an economic power. Although India is seen by some sectors as a competitor vis-à-vis the Philippines, particularly in the business outsourcing industry, this does not overshadow the more positive perception of India as a major source of

---

[73] Chicago Council on Global Affairs, *World Public Opinion 2007: Globalization and Trade, Climate Change, Genocide and Darfur, Future of the United Nations, US Leadership, Rise of China* (Country Highlights: Philippines), p. 79, Ibid.

investments and trade. For example, the Philippine government has also been eyeing India a cheap source of alternative for generic drugs that would help its program of delivering more affordable medicines in the country. In fact, when President Arroyo visited India in October 2007, she encouraged Indian pharmaceutical companies to open up manufacturing plants in the Philippines. During the same visit, it was announced that India will export some US$35 million worth of medicines to the Philippines.[74] Meanwhile, India's controversial patent law served as a model for a recent Philippine law on cheaper medicines that was passed in May 2008 that limits patents on new use of a known substance.[75]

With regard to trade relations with the Philippines, China has become one of the top ten trading partners of the country. In fact, bilateral trade between the two countries dramatically surged between 2000–2007 in favor of the Philippines: from a trade volume of only US$3.14 billion in 2000 to US$30.62 billion in 2007 (which was achieved earlier than targeted in 2010).[76] China is the third major trading partner of the Philippines after the United States and Japan (see Table 1). However, trade relations between the Philippines and India pale in comparison: less than US$1 billion in annual total trade volume between 2002–2007 and has been in the latter's favor (see Table 2).

Apart from trade, other areas of economic cooperation between the Philippines and China are also growing. In January 2007, Premier Wen Jabao signed a US$3.8 billion agricultural project that aims to develop about a million hectares of land in the Philippines to grow rice, corn, and sorghum that could be exported to China. Other agreements

---

[74] Ashok B. Sharma, India, Philippines sign 9 bilateral deals, 5 October 2007, *Financial Express* (India), as reported in bilaterals.org. Available at http://www. bilaterals.org/article.php3?id_article=9867. Accessed on 2 November 2008.

[75] Peter Ollier, Philippines plans to follow India in limiting patentability, 6 May 2008, Managing Intellectual Property. Available at http://www.managingip.com/ Article/1927492/Philippines-plans-to-follow-India-in-limiting-patentability. html. Accessed on 2 November 2008.

[76] Trade between Philippines, Chinese mainland hits record high, 25 January 2008, Xinhua, China Daily. Available at http://www.chinadaily.com.cn/bizchina/ 2008-01/25/content_6421890.htm. Accessed on 2 November 2008.

Table 1: Philippines–China Trade Value (2003–2008)[77] (in US\$ millions)

Year	Export Value (% of total)	Import Value (% of total)	Total Trade (% of total)	Trade Balance +/(−)
2008*	2,974.82 (11.6)	2,142.57 (7.3)	5,117.39 (9.3)	832.25
2007	5,749.86 (11.4)	4,001.23 (7.2)	9,751.10 (9.2)	1,748.63
2006	4,627.66 (9.8)	3,647.35 (7.0)	8,275.01 (8.3)	980.31
2005	4,077.00 (9.9)	2,972.59 (6.3)	7,049.59 (8.0)	1,104.40
2003	2,144.65 (5.92)	1,797.49 (4.79)	3,942.13 (5.35)	347.16

*Data for first half of 2008 only.

Table 2: Philippines–India Trade Value (2000–2007)[78] (in US\$)

Year	Export Value	Import Value	Total Trade	Trade Balance +/(−)
2007*	110,278,554	227,188,012	337,466,566	(116,909,458)
2006	120,130,519	339,556,250	459,686,769	(219,425,731)
2005	86,120,431	344,297,461	430,417,892	(344,297,461)
2004	89,396,414	282,951,620	372,321,034	(193,582,206)
2003	101,853,158	304,291,444	406,144,602	(202,438,286)
2002	89,328,181	428,561,717	517,889,898	(339,233,536)

*Data for 2007 covers only the period of January to June 2007.

include financing for construction of a train line running north of Manila, and rehabilitation of an existing line to the south. To fund the North Rail rehabilitation project, the two countries agreed on a \$500 million loan from the Export and Import Bank of China.[79]

---

[77] Data from Foreign Trade Statistics, Philippine National Statistics Office. http://www.census.gov.ph/data/sectordata/datafts.html. Accessed on 2 November 2008.

[78] "Philippine–India Relations: An Overview," Embassy of the Philippines, New Delhi, India. Available at http://www.newdelhipe.com/philippines-india-relation.html. Accessed on 2 November 2008.

[79] Douglas Bakshian, "Chinese Premier Ends Philippine Visit, After Signing Billions of Dollars in Projects," Voice of America News Com, 16 January 2007. Available at http://www.voanews.com/tibetan/archive/2007-01/2007-01-16-voa2.cfm. Accessed on 1 November 2007.

Notwithstanding the dramatic improvement in bilateral relations between Manila and Beijing, this has been overshadowed since 2007 by a number of political controversies in the Philippines involving Chinese investments. This could very well affect the general public's otherwise positive attitude towards China. Much of this has arosen from allegations of corruption involving Philippine government officials and Chinese companies, such as those related to the ZTE national broadband and the North Rail rehabilitation projects. In particular, the negative publicity generated by the ZTE controversy forced the government to cancel the deal even as it also contributed to the further erosion of President Arroyo's already quite dismal popularity rating. Early in October 2008, opposition groups led by the son of former House Speaker Jose De Venecia filed another impeachment complaint (the fourth since 2005) against President Arroyo partly in connection with the aborted ZTE deal. The elder De Venecia — erstwhile strong ally of President Arroyo — was ousted as House Speaker early in 2008 following his son's expose of alleged bribery scandal in the ZTE deal. His son's company was a losing bidder in the national broadband project.

Meanwhile, the North Rail rehabilitation project funded by the China Export-Import bank worth US$500 million, which was reportedly engineered by the elder De Venecia while he was still House speaker, is allegedly overpriced, was not submitted for public bidding, and did not comply with government rules.[80] These cases no doubt illustrate that China's foreign direct investments and financial assistance have become a major source of corruption in the Philippines. Unlike investments and assistance from more developed countries and multilateral institutions that conform to accountability measures, those from China come with no preconditions, with low interest rates, and long repayment periods. Together with Chinese attitude on financial accountability, they have become a potent mix for corrupt practices in

---

[80] "North Rail Project Faltering Due to Non-Compliance with Rules — Pimentel," Press Release, 14 July 2008, Senate of the Philippines, 14th Congress. Available at http://www.senate.gov.ph/press_release/2008/0714_pimentel1.asp. Accessed on 27 October 2008.

government, which is not only true in the Philippines but also in other developing countries in Southeast Asia.[81]

On political and security relations, significant improvement in Philippine-China ties in this area has been achieved since 2000. In particular, high-level exchange visits have taken place between the two countries since the visit of President Hu in the Philippines in 2005. This includes senior officials from defense and military establishments, as well as legislators from the Philippine Congress. President Gloria Macapagal Arroyo has been making frequent annual visits to China since 2004. In contrast, President Arroyo was on a state visit to India in October 2007, a decade after the visit of former President Fidel V. Ramos. In the meantime, the Philippines and India signed a joint declaration during President Arroyo's visit in New Delhi in 2007 for cooperation in combating international terrorism. This agreement covers exchange of military personnel and students and joint military exercises in non-combat activities.

The expansion of defense and security cooperation between the Philippines and China may be attributed to a number of factors, namely: 1) the desire of the Arroyo administration to become less militarily dependent on the United States, especially in the aftermath of strained relations between Manila and Washington in August 2004 when the Philippines withdrew its humanitarian contingent from Iraq after a Filipino overseas worker was kidnapped; 2) China's attempts to take advantage of this opportunity by exploring an expansion of defense ties with the Philippine military even as it also pushed for joint scientific exploration of the South China Sea with the Philippines and Vietnam; and 3) the general improvement in ASEAN–China relations in the context of ASEAN Plus Three and East Asia Community building projects.

Nonetheless, territorial disputes over the South China Sea between China and other ASEAN claimant states including the Philippines will

---

[81] See Aries Rufo, "Chinese Money Meets Filipino Politics," in Asia Sentinel Consulting, 11 October 2007. Available at http://www.asiasentinel.com/index.php?Itemid=31&id=758&option=com_content&task=view. Accessed on 27 October 2008.

continue to be a source of tension, notwithstanding attempts by China, the Philippines, and Vietnam to undertake joint resource exploration in the area. The three-year Joint Marine Seismic Understanding (JMSU) agreement signed by the three countries in 2005 expired in July 2008 and has not been extended.[82] Apparently, the Philippine government simply decided to have the agreement lapse amidst reported increasing pressures from China for the Philippine Congress to abandon attempts to pass the country's archipelagic baseline law before the United Nations Convention on the Law of Sea (UNCLOS) expires in May 2009. The Arroyo administration and some legislators are apparently not in sync on the urgency of passing the baseline law, which will cover the areas claimed by the Philippines in the South China Sea.[83]

Southeast Asia and "soft power" capabilities of China and India

So much has been said about the competing interests of China and India in Southeast Asia. Their rise as regional powers with the ability to influence events and developments in this part of the word is something that cannot be taken for granted. At the same time, there are also expectations in ASEAN that their emergence should contribute to development, peace, and stability of the region instead of undermining these. Hence, it is important to raise questions about China's and India's "soft power" capabilities. That it should not only enhance their positive image but also, in the long term, develop the confidence of states and peoples in Southeast Asia that these rising powers will be responsible stakeholders are fundamental expectations. More specifically, would China and India be willing to contribute more to help

---

[82] Abigail Ho, RP-China-Vietnam exploration deal in Spratlys lapses, 11 July 2008, *Philippine Daily Inquirer* online. Available at http://newsinfo.inquirer. net/inquirerheadlines/nation/view/20080711-147739/RP-China-Vietnam-exploration-deal-on-Spratlys-lapses. Accessed on 11 July 2008.

[83] Benjamin B. Pulta, RP risks war with China on Spratlys baseline bill, 24 April 2008, *The Daily Tribune* online. Available at http://www.tribune.net.ph/20080424/headlines/20080424hed1.html. Accessed on 2 November 2008.

promote human security and human development in Southeast Asia? Are they willing to help ASEAN, for example, in narrowing the development gap not only between the old and new members but also within each developing members?

In the case of China, for instance, will it continue to practice resource extraction diplomacy towards developing countries of ASEAN, without regard to human security, good governance, and human development concerns in these countries? Would China's energy security priorities that forced it to build huge dams in the Three Gorges undermine the environmental security of its Southeast Asian neighbors, especially those along the downstream areas of the Mekong? Will China continue to support the military junta in Myanmar in order to secure access to the country's raw materials and energy resources? In the same vein, are China's efforts to pursue joint resource exploration with the Philippines and Vietnam in the South China Sea lead to better management of the area as a "commons" or would it further complicate sovereignty claims in the area? As a rising economic and military power with growing energy and resource needs, China has to allay the concerns of its neighbors on these issues. A more conventional response to these questions would simply highlight the pragmatic approach that China usually takes in dealing with these issues. Yet one cannot also ignore the fact that Beijing is not immune from international criticisms and would adjust accordingly its foreign policy responses to such. Ultimately, it has to balance its narrow, practical interests vis-à-vis its long-term goal of acquiring legitimacy as a major power. To date, both rising powers have not contributed as much to addressing these human security concerns, compared to Japan and the United States for example.

Just like China, India's growing energy requirements have also forced it to venture into resource extraction diplomacy in many parts of Africa, Latin America, and also in Southeast Asia. Specifically, in Myanmar and Vietnam, Indian national oil companies have acquired oil and natural gas exploration blocks as part of building its strategic energy reserves.[84] Given this strategic interest, India has also increased

---

[84] Ingolf Kiesow and Nicklas Norling, The Rise of India: Problems and Opportunities, pp. 98–99.

military aid to the Myanmar junta since 2005, and initiatives for joint cooperation in dealing with counter-insurgency operations along their common border have been proposed.[85] Interestingly, although India is a democratic state, it has refrained just like China from criticizing the ruling junta in Myanmar on human rights and domestic political issues.

Overall, the resource extraction diplomacy of China and India towards some countries in the region raises questions about their "soft power" capabilities especially in the area of promoting human security, good governance, and human development. No doubt, their preference to hide behind "non-intervention" principles has served their pragmatic interests quite well. Sooner or later, however, both powers would have to face any backlash that results from their policies that are not based on the promotion of good governance. Recent developments in the Philippines, for example, have exposed China's business practices that were perceived to have contributed to worsening level of corruption in government, which consequently undermined China's image in the country. In 2007, a senior American diplomat criticized China for being a source of corruption in Cambodia, Laos, and Myanmar as it reportedly provided large amounts of money to build infrastructure that are aimed at encouraging Chinese trade and businesses in the region.[86]

Meanwhile, India's policy towards Myanmar is basically a balancing act between its geopolitical interests and its commitment to democracy. Despite criticisms from Indian opposition parties and some Burmese in exile in India, New Delhi is expected to pursue quiet diplomacy and constructive engagement with the junta in Myanmar. For one, India is afraid that open criticism of the junta will only push Naypidaw closer to China. The Indian armed forces also needs the cooperation of the

---

[85] Gideon Lundhold, Pipeline Politics: India and Myanmar, from PINR (Power and Interest News Report), 10 September 2007. Available at http://www.pinr.com/report.php?ac=view_report&report_id=679&language_id=1. Accessed on 18 August 2008.

[86] "U.S. diplomat says China's influence in Southeast Asia is unproductive," The Associated Press, 27 July 2007. Available at KI-Media, http://ki-media.blogspot.com/2007/07/us-diplomat-china-is-source-of.html. Accessed on 18 August 2008.

Myanmar junta in dealing with insurgency problems along their common border.[87] To New Delhi's credit, it has quietly stopped all arms sales and transfers to Myanmar in late December 2007 even as it also supported the UN Human Rights Council's resolution condemning the violent crackdown by the military junta against Buddhist monks.[88]

Exploring cooperation in non-traditional security issues

Notwithstanding certain concerns as enumerated above, the rise of China and India could also be viewed as a good opportunity for closer cooperation with ASEAN in the area non-traditional security (NTS) issues. Specifically, both powers could provide assistance to many ASEAN countries in the dealing with problems related to maritime security, drug trafficking, natural disasters, pandemic diseases (HIV/AIDS and avian flu), ethnic conflicts, environmental threats, and counter-terrorism, among others. China, for example, has expressed great concern over the drug trafficking from Myanmar to the Chinese province of Yunnan. This transnational issue has also fueled drug addiction, crime, and the spread of HIV/AIDS in that part of China.[89] A similar problem along the India–Myanmar border has been reported, which also includes arms smuggling and other types of illegal cross-border trade. Complicating this problem are armed anti-Indian insurgency groups based inside Myanmar (e.g. United Liberation Front of Asom, United National Liberation Front, and National Socialist Council of Nagaland), which have been tolerated by the military junta

---

[87] Uday Bhanu Singh, Recent Developments in Myanmar, 2 November 2007, IDSA Strategic Comments, Institute for Defense Studies & Analyses. Available at http://www.idsa.in/publications/stratcomments/UdaiBhanuSingh021107.htm. Accessed on 18 August 2008.

[88] Brian McCartan, Myanmar deal right neighborly of India, 11 January 2008, *Asia Times Online*. Available at http://www.atimes.com/atimes/Southeast_Asia/JA11Ae01.html. Accessed on 18 August 2008.

[89] Ian Storey, Burma's Relations with China: Neither Puppet Nor Pawn, *China Brief*, Vol. 7, Issue No. 3 (7 February 2007). Available at http://www.jamestown.org/china_brief/article.php?articleid=2373268. Accessed on 18 August 2008.

and used as a bargaining chip vis-à-vis India.[90] Burmese refugees flee-ing into India and Thailand have also caused some ethnic tensions and communal violence in border areas of these host countries.

Cooperating with ASEAN on these NTS issues not only puts pres-sure on developing member states, including Myanmar, to address basic human development and human security issues. It also encourages both China and India to do more in providing assistance to these countries to address the root causes of NTS problems, such as poverty and creating opportunities for greater access to basic services. Although China and India are still faced with similar problems, they could very well provide developing countries of ASEAN with technical and financial assistance that directly address these human security problems. Both powers could also provide training for local government officials in some ASEAN countries in building their capacities to address these issues. India and China could also participate together in maritime security cooperation with ASEAN, not just under the bilateral ASEAN-China and ASEAN-India frameworks. Both China and ASEAN have already developed frameworks and mechanisms for cooperation in dealing with NTS, such as the Shanghai Cooperation Organization (SCO) and the ASEAN Regional Forum (ARF), where India is already a participant.

Breaking the impasse in Myanmar

While China and India clearly have their respective geopolitical and strategic reasons for not directly interfering in the internal affairs of Myanmar, this does not preclude them from supporting the call of ASEAN and the rest of the international community for that country to move towards national reconciliation and democratization. The current political impasse in Myanmar essentially demonstrates the need for innovative and alternative approaches to constructive engagement as well as ineffective sanctions imposed by the West. Both have failed in bringing about political change in the country. If anything, the violent crackdown against monks and their democratic supporters in September 2007 and the humanitarian crisis brought about by cyclone

---

[90] Brian McCartan, Ibid.

Nargis in May 2008 indicate that the core leaders of the military junta continue to be out of sync with the suffering of the Burmese people.

ASEAN has not been successful in dealing with the junta in Myanmar and could even face further embarrassment once the ASEAN Charter gets to be ratified by all member states. This is so because without provisions in the Charter for sanctions against erring members, Myanmar could simply ignore pressures from ASEAN over the long run. Even the vague provisions about creating a human rights body is likely to be blocked by the military junta, along with new and conservative members that are wary of interference by other countries, particularly on human rights issues. However, given the considerable degree of influence that China and India have in Myanmar, both powers could facilitate — through quiet and backdoor diplomacy — dialogue between the junta and democratic leaders in the country. ASEAN's experience in dealing with the Cambodian conflict in the 1980s should serve as an important guidepost for working towards ending the impasse in Myanmar. Specifically, until China and other major powers (such as Japan, France, and the former Soviet Union) were willing and able to contribute towards breaking the political stalemate in Cambodia, no initiative of ASEAN on the political settlement of the issue took off. Thus, China and India could play a critical role in breaking the stalemate in Myanmar. An important consideration in this regard is the willingness of both powers to cooperate with ASEAN and the international community in effectively reducing military assistance to the junta, which India had already done since the end of 2007. At the same time, China and India could increase their level of humanitarian assistance to the country, which could help alleviate the serious level of human suffering in Myanmar. This effort, in partnership with ASEAN members, need not be confined to official transactions but could also involve a number of civil society and humanitarian organizations in the region.

Norm building and East Asia community

China and India as emerging powers cannot ignore the importance of the normative dimension of international relations. Southeast Asia and the larger East Asian region are composed of countries with a wide range of variation in terms of political systems, level of economic development, and social-cultural norms. These factors may or may not contribute to community building in the region, depending on how national leaders and relevant sectors play up their respective importance. What is crucial, however, is whether political elites have the will and commitment to build a common identity, despite the reality of existing diversities. The norms and principles already enshrined in several declarations of ASEAN, the ARF, ASEAN Plus Three, and the East Asian Summit (EAS) are important starting points for building a regional identity, at least among political elites. (While India as a major power is not yet substantively involved in some of these frameworks, its increasing level of engagement with ASEAN through binding agreements could rope it in within the process of community building in the region as well.) How these norms and principles are internalized and successfully passed on to the next generation of future leaders in East Asia is something that must be ensured if one must be convinced that indeed the ASEAN Community and East Asian Community ideas are indeed serious projects.

Community building involves the transformation of the regional order and the institutionalization of norms, principles, and habits of consultation would certainly be a long process. If the political elites of East Asia are serious about taking charge of shaping the region's future, they have to pay attention to building a common identity based on developing a set of common values and norms of engagement in dealing with traditional and non-traditional security issues. Major powers like China and India, along with Japan, could contribute towards this end by overcoming their historical baggage or animosities and start focusing on how to begin writing a common future history for peoples and states of the region. However, these major powers must also exercise restraint and demonstrate responsible behavior in the way that they relate with smaller countries in this part of the world.

Conclusion

The rise of China and India should not be seen solely in the context of zero-sum game or balance of power rivalry. ASEAN should not let this "realist" framework determine or constrain its ability to engage these emerging powers to play a more positive role and for them to become responsible stakeholders in the region. While hedging may be a good strategy for ASEAN states in dealing with these emerging powers, it is also important not to lose sight of more fundamental human security concerns that are also shared by China and India. At the end of the day, the security of states could only be ensured if human security issues are dealt with accordingly. Given the pragmatic approaches that both rising powers have adopted in dealing with traditional and non-traditional security issues in the region, it may take a long while before China and India could become more comfortable with employing their respective reservoir of "soft power" vis-à-vis Southeast Asian countries. Internal economic priorities and domestic political constraints are likely to shape their policies towards the region.

Chapter 5

Negotiating the Rise of Asia — A Perspective from Malaysia's Relations with India and China

Johan Saravanamuttu

Introduction

The economic and political ascendancy of Asia is an apparent truism, yet the manner in which the rise of Asia has occurred in discursive terms, if not in reality, surely merits further analysis. A signature discourse in the literature came by way of a book entitled, *The Voice of Asia*, jointly written by Mahathir Mohamad and Shintaro Ishihara (1995). As the sleeve of the book flamboyantly puts it, "The future belongs to Asia...two of the most prominent outspoken proponents of an Asian model of capitalism challenge Western domination and celebrate the renaissance of the region's ancient civilizations". The book came close on the heels of S.P. Huntington's *Clash of Civilization* (1993), which suggested that Asian civilization(s) were in collision course with the West. Mahathir and Ishihara's underlying thesis was rather that Asian values and culture was actually superior to those of the West and that would ultimately explain Asia's invariable economic ascendancy and prosperity. Kishore Mahbubani (2008) takes the thesis even further by arguing that there is already an irresistible shift of global power to

the East or Asia. He is careful to add though that Asia wants to repli-
cate, not dominate the West.[91]

A counterpoint to the discourse of Asian economic and political
ascendancy comes from a large array of scholars in the West, who have
re-scripted the idea of American hegemony, which at least major two
authors, if not more, have argued also evince attributes of "empire".[92]
Cambridge and Harvard luminary Niall Ferguson suggests that while
somewhat tattered here and there, the American "Colossus" nonetheless still dominates the trajectory of global transformations while Amy
Chua of Yale propounds the thesis that the "hyperpower", which the US
is, like the empires of old, cannot be culturally intolerant with
impunity. The suggestion it seems would be that a culturally more
savvy American empire would continue to dominate the world for eons.
So how does one resolve this apparent contradiction in the literature?
More specifically, how does this apparent contradiction get resolved in
a paper that purports to deal with the rise of China and India from the
perspective of a medium-sized Asian country like Malaysia?

In this paper, I would take it that "hegemonic stability" is an
imperative of the current phase of globalization[93] and that the United
States being the world's sole superpower provides such "stability"
given its global reach. Economic growth and prosperity is of course
another sort of question and it seems undeniable merely from staring
at statistics and economic data that Asia, generally speaking, is on the

---

[91] See Mahbubani (2008) who seems to be saying that a "de-Westenization" is
still largely premised on the well-trodden modern ideals such as "new instincts
of cultural tolerance and understanding" (p. 173). The main point of the book,
as I read it, is to critique Western "incompetence" rather than say, Western
enlightenment thought, including American "pragmatism" which Asia has or
should adopt (Chapters 5 and 6). See also Asad Latif for a Singapore
perspective (2008) on India's rise. For a counterpoint to the hype about Asia's
rise, see Stubbs (2005).

[92] See Ferguson (2005) and Chua (2007).

[93] The debate about globalization in the international relations literature is
ongoing. I will adopt by and large the perspective of Robert Gilpin (2001, see
especially pp. 93–97). For a recent critical take on the globalization debate, see
the volume by Veltmeyer (2008).

ascendancy. Whether this presages a necessary Western decline remains moot. A further point to be made is that hegemonic stability could also be decomposed regionally and clearly major powers like China and India, and, possibly Japan, play the role of a steadying hand in maintaining regional order, in East Asia, if not the Asia Pacific.[94] Within such a frame of analysis, now enter the economically ascendant small and medium level states of Asia. Malaysia would be such a state. Thus, it is necessary for Malaysia, as a 'middle power' to 'negotiate' its relations to the optimal level with the likes of regional hegemons such as China or India as much as it would need to position itself against a superpower like the US or extra-regional grouping like the European Union. Such negotiation of foreign policy and foreign relations must naturally take into account shared mutual interests. This chapter will try to illustrate how that has occurred in the last four or five decades.

Positioning Towards China and India

Let me first briefly touch on Malaysia's conjoined history with China and India. Without going too far back in time it does not take much to realise that Malaysia as modern nation-state owes much to historical ties with China and India. Particularly important was the transformation of the Malayan Peninsula and Sabah and Sarawak into its present social and political configuration during the British period. The very presence of the large minorities of Chinese and Indians in Malaysia was the result of a colonial economy and administration. So much has been written about Malayan colonial history that there is no need to rehearse this here except suffice it to say that Malaysian post-colonial relations with China and India were thereby greatly influence by its Chinese and Indian populations. Moreover, British colonial rule also directly linked India and Malaya when the British India Office for a time administered the Straits Settlements of Penang, Malacca and Singapore before they became crown colonies in 1867.

---

[94] I am excluding for the moment the role of regional blocs or groupings like ASEAN or APEC.

Malaysia's first prime minister, Tunku Abdul Rahman showed a particular political affinity towards India. The Tunku government condemned in the strongest terms the Chinese occupation of Tibet in 1959 and launched a "Save Democracy Fund in 1962 when hostilities broke out between Indian and China in their respective borders.[95] Malaysia's stand at the UN was unequivocal that China had started "unprovoked aggression on India".[96] The whole episode should of course be cast in the context of the Cold War and Malaysia as I have argued elsewhere had clearly located itself on the anti-communism side of the divide, which clearly the fueled by the insurgency led by the China-inspired Malayan Communist Party. Furthermore at that point of time Malaysia had not diplomatic relations with the People's Republic of China and Tunku showed partiality to Taiwan by allowing it to set up a small consular office in Kuala Lumpur.[97]

By the 1970s, while Malaysia's relations with India remained on an even keel, much began to move vis-à-vis China. No adjustments were evidently needed for Malaysia–India relations while a major change in China relations occurred in 1971 when Malaysia voted for the Albanian resolution allowing for the seating of China and, consequently, Taiwan's expulsion. There followed in October 1971, a 19-man Trade Mission to China, led by Pernas (Perbadanan Nasional or National Corporation) Chairman, Tengku Razaleigh, to establish direct trade links with the People's Republic. Subsequent missions followed, paving the way for unofficial negotiations on recognition and diplomatic ties. The most important of these negotiations were carried out, it was revealed later, in secret meetings between the Malaysian UN Representative at New York, Zakaria Mohd Ali, and his Chinese counterpart, Huang Hua.[98] The two men had first met in Ottawa when they were ambassadors to Canada. The Chinese position at these meetings was that diplomatic relations should come first while Malaysia wanted the outstanding issues settled before ties could be

---

[95] The Fund raised one million Malaysian dollars.
[96] Saravanamuttu (1983, p. 27).
[97] Ibid., p. 26.
[98] See Zakaria Mohd Ali's own account of his role in Fauziah M. Taib (2006, pp. 119–130).

formalised (Noordin Sopiee, 1974: 50). From the Malaysian perspective, there were three main issues (a) China's support for the Malayan Communist Party (MCP), (b) the related question of "Suara Revolusi Malaya" (Malayan Voice of Revolution) radio broadcasts which emanated from China and, (c) the status of the 220,000 stateless Chinese in Malaysia. China, apparently after a little hesitation, agreed to discuss these and other issues and by December's end, agreement had been reached on the entire range of questions.[99] As a prelude to the China ties, Malaysia had recognised without much fanfare the Mongolian Republic, North Vietnam, North Korea and East Germany within 1972–1973.

On May 27, 1974, a Malaysian entourage, led by Prime Minister Tun Abdul Razak, left for the People's Republic of China in the first high-level official contact of the two governments since Malaya's independence in 1957. On May 31, Malaysia and China announced the normalisation of relations to be followed by an exchange of ambassadors. At the same time, Malaysia terminated diplomatic (consular) relations with Taiwan. In the joint communiqué announcing the normalisation of relations, the two governments agreed on the following chief points:

> [T]hat although the social systems of the People's Republic of China and Malaysia are different, this should not constitute an obstacle to the two Governments and people in establishing and developing peaceful and friendly relations between the two countries on the basis of the principles of mutual respect for sovereignty and territorial integrity, mutual non-aggression, non-interference in each other's internal affairs, equality and mutual benefit, and peaceful co-existence. The two Governments consider all foreign aggression, interference, control and subversion to be impermissible. They hold that the social system of

---

[99] Zakaria Mohd Ali made clear, from his account of the negotiations cited above, that the two most important issues for Malaysia was the Communist insurgency and the overseas Chinese question. Recognition of the sovereign state of Malaysia implied the non-support of the MCP while China's rejection of dual citizenship resolved the status of Malaysia's stateless Chinese. For China, as Zakaria points out, the crucial issue was that Malaysia acknowledged that Taiwan was part of China (see ibid, p. 129).

a country should be chosen and decided by its own people. They are opposed to any attempt by any country or group or countries to establish hegemony or create spheres of influence in any part of the world.[100]

Specifically, Malaysia stated that it recognised "the Government of the People's Republic of China as the sole legal Government of China and acknowledges the position of the Chinese Government that Taiwan is an inalienable part of the territory of the People's Republic of China". The Chinese Government, on its part took note that Malaysia is a multiracial country with people of Malay, Chinese and other ethnic origins. Both the Government of the People's Republic of China and the Government of Malaysia declared that they did not recognise dual nationality. Proceeding from this principle, the Chinese Government considered anyone of Chinese origin who had taken up of his own will or acquiring Malaysian nationality as automatically forfeiting Chinese nationality. Although not specifically mentioned in the joint *communiqué*, it seemed that China was prepared to stop actively supporting the MCP and base its relations with Malaysia on the five Bandung principles of co-existence. At any rate, it appeared to be the Malaysian government's understanding that "non-interference" in internal affairs was a reference to the MCP issue. Thus the Malaysian Prime Minister said on his return that he had 'received assurances in private talks with both Chairman Mao and Premier Chou that the MCP was Malaysia's "internal problem".[101]

China also accepted Malaysia's position on the issue of overseas Chinese (*Hua Chiao*), which is based on the principles of *jus soli*. In the

---

[100] Retrieved from *Foreign Affairs Malaysia*, 7 (1974), pp. 52–53.

[101] Ibid., pp. 56–57. These "assurances" did not, however, prevent the People's Republic from sending a congratulatory message to the MCP in April 1975, a little over a year after the establishment of diplomatic relations. Malaysia protested the Chinese action and said that relations would not remain as "cordial" if the practice continued. The episode did not however, trigger a serious strain in ties, the' Chinese action being probably routine rather that premeditated.

past, China applied the principle of *jus sanguinis* in the fear that Taiwan would absorb the *Hua Chiao* if the local societies rejected them. As a *quid pro quo* to the concessions made by China, Malaysia discarded its ambivalent stand on Taiwan in stating plainly that the island was an inalienable part of the People's Republic of China and in so doing also breaking off ties with the island republic. Premier Chou also spoke favourably, if only generally, of the Malaysian–ASEAN scheme for the neutralisation of Southeast Asia. In his words, "... the Malaysian Government's position for the establishment of a Zone of Peace and Neutrality in Southeast Asia gives expression to the desire of the Southeast Asian People to shake off foreign interference and control (and) has won support from many Third World countries".

The China visit was a diplomatic breakthrough for Malaysia and a personal triumph for Tun Razak. The diplomatic coup was also used to great advantage by the Razak government in the 1974 General Election. It was common knowledge that the use of posters showing Razak shaking hands with Mao during the election campaign period won the hearts and votes of Malaysian Chinese. Thus with the establishment of diplomatic ties with the People's Republic of China, Malaysia's foreign diplomacy had more or less come around full circle. It could now claim with greater credibility to have a non-aligned foreign policy and thereby pursue a policy of equidistance *vis-à-vis* the major powers. As long as it did not recognize China and China did not recognize Malaysia, such a strategy of equidistance, *ipso facto*, could not be pursued.

For Malaysia, the China recognition had multiple salutary effects. Malaysia's scheme of the neutralization of Southeast Asia and its notion of a Zone of Peace Freedom and Neutrality (ZOPFAN), first floated in 1971 as the Kuala Lumpur Declaration gained momentum. ZOPFAN later became a flagship policy of the Association of Southeast Asian Nations (ASEAN), which also impelled ASEAN to establish the Southeast Asian Nuclear Weapons Free Zone (SEANWFZ) in 1994. The latter scheme has received China's explicit support.

In contrast to China, Malaysia's relations with India have been very cordial and close throughout the years, with Malaysia even showing some degree of partiality to the Asian subcontinental power.

Malaysian primes ministers have visited India on many occasions; Hussein Onn in 1979 and 1980 (for CHOGM[102]), Mahathir in 1983 (NAM[103] Summit), 1993 (aborted G-15 meeting), 1994 (G-15 Summit), and in 1996 to receive the Jawaharlal Nehru Award for International Understanding. Indian presidents on their part have also made many visits to Malaysia as have Indian prime ministers Pandit Nehru, Indira Ghandi, V.P. Singh, Narasimha Rao and Atal Bihari Vajpayee. In 1990, it was officially agreed to upgrade the official Joint Committee to that of a Joint Commissions headed by foreign ministers of both sides. India's commercial involvement in Malaysia has been consistent and particularly impressive in the IT field, with 36 Indian companies participating in Malaysia's Mulitmedia Super Corridor.[104] The pattern of cordial relations was recently affected by the HINDRAF[105] rally in Kuala Lumpur on November 25, 2007 which saw the detention under Malaysia's internal security law of five HINDRAF leaders. One of the HINDRAF leaders escaped arrest and travelled to India to seek international support for the cause of the alleged 'marginalization' of the Indian community in Malaysia. The issue was raised in the Indian Parliament (upper and lower houses) in February of 2008. At the peak of the episode, the Indian Premier Manmohan Singh sought an explanation from the Malaysian government but this was not until unsavoury exchanges occurred between Malaysian government spokespersons and Indian politicians such as Tamil Nadu chief minister M. Karunanidhi.[106] The episode clearly shows that the large Indian minority in Malaysia does have an impact on Malaysia–India relationships and that the Malaysian government cannot afford to short-shrift Malaysian Indians with impunity.

---

[102] Commonwealth Heads of Government Meeting.

[103] Nonaligned Movement.

[104] These facts are drawn from India's Ministry of External Affairs webpage, http://meaindia.nic.in/

[105] Hindu Rights Action Force.

[106] Minister in the Prime Minister's Department Nazri Abdul Aziz provoked an outcry when he asked the Tamil Nadu Chief Minister to "lay off" Malaysian internal affairs. (From various news reports).

Malaysia's overall positioning between China and India through to the 1970s was perhaps still skewed toward a notion of a "China threat" and a worry about India's partiality to the Soviet Union, which was considered hostile to the region in Malaysian thinking. Malaysia was able to use the rhetoric of nonalignment to balance relations between the two Asian powers, which clearly were in rivalry, given their different policies toward the Soviet Union, let alone the US. For most of the mid till the end of the 1970s, Malaysia was preoccupied with relations with the Indochina states and the ramifications of the end of the Vietnam War. In particular Malaysia was among a number of Southeast states that bore the brunt of the influx of boat refugees from Vietnam. In 1980, Prime Minister Hussein Onn, together with President Suharto of Indonesia, proclaimed the so-called "Kuantan Doctrine". Believing that Vietnamese action was in part motivated by its mistrust of China, President Suharto and Premier Hussein Onn met at Kuantan, Pahang and put forward a proposal which called for Vietnam to move to a position of neutrality between China and the Soviet Union. The doctrine was declared with an eye toward the Cambodian impasse which fuelled the China–Vietnam rivalry and implied a Soviet involvement.[107] With the resolution of the Cambodian conflict by the early 1990s, Malaysia's relations with China become much more stabilised.

China, India and the Look East Policy, 1980s–1990s

For period from 1981 until the end of the 1990s, Malaysian foreign policy was under the watch of Mahathir Mohamed. Both India and China did not appear to feature prominently for most part of Mahathir's early foreign relations. Instead, the Commonwealth, which Mahathir considered to be a colonial legacy was snubbed by the Malaysian premier who then turned his attention to Japan in particular in his proclamation of the "Look East" policy. This was the policy of emulating the

---

[107] See Gyngell (1982, p. 133).

economic model and work ethic of the Japanese. The Malaysian public was bombarded with a relentless barrage of propaganda about "the Japanese miracle". Clearly it was politically less expedient to emulate Chinese-dominant Singapore nor could Taiwan or Hong Kong serve as ideal models despite Mahathir's rhetoric about the new economic "dragons"; Japan was still his model *par excellence*.[108] As I have argued elsewhere, and to mix a metaphor, the whole idea of the Look East Policy dovetailed well with the "flying geese" pattern of development in the East Asian region promoted by Japan.[109] In the early 1990s, Mahathir took his Look East Policy a step further by proposing the East Asian Economic Grouping (EAEG), which later was changed to the East Asian Economic Caucus (EAEC). The EAEG/EAEC was the logical outcome of an enlarged ASEAN. Mahathir said that his idea was not new since South Korea had in 1970 proposed the Asian Common Market while Japan's Ministry of International Trade and Industry suggested an "Asian Network" in 1988. China was naturally included in the EAEG scheme, but not India. As enunciated by Mahathir:

> The EAEG or EAEC should neither be a formal grouping like ASEAN nor should it be a trade bloc like NAFTA or the EC. As it is dedicated to world free trade, it cannot be protectionist and give its members preferential treatment in intra-regional trade. Its chief purpose is to provide a strong voice for East Asian countries in trade negotiations with the rest of world, particularly the EC and NAFTA. It has been obvious for a long time that no one respects the voices of developing countries like Malaysia, or even of groups like ASEAN. But a regional forum with China, Japan together with the ASEAN six as members will have a much

---

[108] However, the policy of emulation was extended to South Korea, sealed through scholarships and exchanges just as with Japan, which proffered "Mombushu" scholarships to Malaysians. One could well surmise why two other Chinese-populated NICs, Taiwan, with no diplomatic ties with Malaysia, and Hong Kong, not an independent state, were not accorded the same privilege as South Korea.

[109] See Saravanamuttu (1998).

greater clout if they speak with one voice on common problems affecting them". (*New Straits Times,* 15 October 1992).

Mahathir's idea met headlong with American opposition and a lukewarm Japanese response as both states were then promoting the larger more encompassing Asia Pacific Economic Cooperation (APEC) grouping. Australia took umbrage when Mahathir said it should be excluded from the EAEC. There was little or no reaction to Mahathir's proposal on the part of China, and also India, which at this point seemed automatically excluded from notions of 'East Asian' regionalism. It could perhaps be said that Mahathir's notion of East Asian regionalism did ultimately influence ASEAN's creation of the ASEAN Plus Three grouping, which involves China, and the East Asian Summit, which includes India. The rivalry and undertone of conflict between China–Japan and China–India no doubt affected how Malaysia positioned itself vis-à-vis these three major Asian states.

Under Mahathir, it would appear that East Asian regionalism could have been used as a bridge to ameliorate the differences between Japan and China, although India hardly ever came into the equation. This said, Japanese ties to the US along with overt Mahathirian aversion to US political and economic presence in the region tended to forestall such a progression. Mahathir's notion of hooking up with Japan was premised mainly on Japanese economic presence and clout in the region and its role in the flying geese pattern of development, which entailed a regional division of labour in capitalist development with Japan as the leader of the flock. China's lower economic profile and Malaysia's overall perception of it as a Communist state meant it could hardly play a similar role to that of Japan, at least up till the late 1990s.

Security Issues

In the security issue-area, Malaysia's frictions with China tended to be rather prominent due to contending territorial claims in the South China Sea. Malaysia began to assume a slightly confrontational stance towards China after it published its new territorial map in 1979. Malaysia has up till now occupied five disputed reefs and islets of the

Spratlys in the South China Sea.[110] In June 1983, Malaysia reportedly deployed 20 commandos to Terumbu Layang Layang (Swallow Reef) which drew a protest from China's Foreign Ministry, which argued that "China has indisputable sovereignty over the Nanshah Islands and the nearby waters and that the natural resources *n* these areas belong to China".[111] Defence analyst Razak Baginda (2002) suggests that China's attitude towards most claimants to the Spratly group of island is one of posturing rather than a real military threat. The Mischief Reef incident of 1995 was thought to have targeted Vietnam to which China evidently has a more bellicose posture. The fact that Malaysia's occupation of five reefs has seen no ostensible military reaction from Beijing suggests a softer line towards Kuala Lumpur.

In contrast to China, there has been continuing security and defence cooperation between Malaysia and India. Defence cooperation including exchanges and military training were began during the Mahathir years with the signing of an MOU in 1993. The Malaysia–Indian Defence Cooperation Meetings (MIDCOM) followed. There were four MIDCOM meetings held until 2002. The third MIDCOM held in January 2001 witnessed the setting up of the sub-committees on cooperation in the military, defence industry and science and technology sectors. Two important sub-committees were the Sub-Committee for Military Cooperation (SCMC) and the Indian Technical and Economic Cooperation (ITEC) programme. Malaysian military personnel have received training in India under the latter programme. During the January 2007 visit to Kuala Lumpur of Indian Defence Minister Mr. A.K. Antony for talks with the Malaysian Defence Minister, it was reported that the two countries discussed and sealed a number of important collaborations. These included training to Malaysian

---

[110] Former Foreign Minister Syed Hamid revealed that Malaysia had 15 claims in the Spratly group of islands and had occupied five of them, including Terumbu Layang-Layang since 1983, the Ubi and Mantanani atolls (1986) and the Siput and Peninjau atolls (1999). In Layang-Layang, Malaysia has built a 3-star resort known as Swallow Reefs popular with nature lovers. See Jeshurun (2007, p. 236).

[111] As cited by Abdul Razak Baginda (2002, p. 237).

personnel at various levels including at the National Defence College and Staff College, high-level exchange of visits, visit of ships of the two navies, and India's regular participation in Langkawi International Maritime and Aerospace (LIMA) exhibition. Both the countries have also participated in exercises like the bilateral PASSEX and the multi-lateral MILAN. The two countries in November 2007 signed a Protocol on training of Royal Malaysian Air Force (RMAF) pilots by Indian Air Force on SU-30 MKM aircraft. Earlier in May 2007, an MoU was signed by Hindustan Aeronautics Limited with the Malaysian Ministry of Defence for the technical training of RMAF personnel on SU-30 MKM aircraft.[112]

Managing the China–India Ascendancy

By the end of the 1990s, Malaysia had made important political over-tures to China in the aftermath of the 1997–98 Asian financial crisis. In August 1999, in a speech in Beijing at the Third Malaysia–China Forum, Prime Minister Mahathir alluded to the common stances the two countries had taken and called for both nations "to work with each other East Asian Countries to urge develop nations for a concerted effort to create a new global financial architecture" (Razak Baginda, 2002, p. 243). Towards the later part of Mahathir's tenure a few signif-icant moves were also made in the economic arena to India and China such as the offer to participate in the RM14.5 billion 329 km double-tracking railway project running between Ipoh and Padang Besar. The project which was awarded to then Malaysian Mining Corporation (MMC) and the Gamuda companies was temporarily shelved when Abdullah Badawi which took over the helm of government at the end of 2003. Reportedly, the Abdullah administration revived the project in 2007 and started negotiations soon after with MMC and Gamuda for the northern section while the southern section, running from

---

[112] From various news reports. The extension of defence and other collabora-tions, including the signing of an FTA with Malaysia, was in keeping with India's own "Look East" policy. See, for example, reports by AFP, *Xinhua* and *Bernama*, January 7, 2008.

Seremban to Gemas, has been awarded to Indian Railway Construction Co (IRCON), the construction arm of Indian Railways, and a local company.[113]

An interesting geo-strategic move by Prime Minister Abdullah was his June 2004 visit to China, ahead of both his US and Japan visits. Over the years, Malaysia has become ASEAN's largest trading partner with China with a massive USD20 billion in two-way trade in 2003 (*People's Daily Online*, June 1, 2004). Abdullah's visit also commemorated the 30th anniversary of diplomatic ties with China important as a statement itself given Malaysia's large Chinese population and the fact that it was the first ASEAN country to recognize the People's Republic of China in 1974. However, relations with China took a rude knock in November and December 2005 in what has come to be known as "the nude ear squat incident".[114] The incident began when the Democratic Action Party (DAP) member of parliament Teresa Kok alleged that police had sexually outraged a woman who was a Chinese national, also making her do ear squats. Other reports of similar abuses then started to surface. An anonymous whistle blower then produced a video depicting a female police officer ordering a female detainee (later identified as a Malay woman) to perform ear squats in the nude. A public inquiry was instituted with regard to the video incident and clearly the suggestion that Chinese nationals were short-shrifted by Malaysian authorities created enough flak to send home minister Azmi Khalid to Beijing on 5 December to mend fences with China. Azmi explained that his visit was meant to explain several matters related to the perception of the public and government there regarding immigration enforcement issues and other enforcement on Chinese tourists in Malaysia. Earlier on 29 November, deputy internal security minister Noh Omar had made the unfortunate remark that if foreigners thought that Malaysian police

---

[113] However, up till the time of writing, there appears to be little movement on the double tracking project. Instead, some new reports surfaced that the Malaysian company YTL Corporation is proposing a bullet train from Kuala Lumpur to Singapore. This appears to be different to the double tracking project.
[114] Based on various newspaper reports and those of internet paper Malaysiakini.com.

were brutal, they should go back to their own countries and not stay in Malaysia.[115] There appears to be ambivalence on the part of the Malaysian government toward the nude squat issue; on the one hand, it did not want to offend China for geo-political and economic reasons but, at the same time, the Malay leadership seemed to want to resist local Chinese oppositional pressure over the issue.

Prime Minister Abdullah made a trip to India in December 2004 where he received an honorary doctorate from the Jamia Millia Islamia University, his first from a foreign institution of higher learning for his promotion of Islam *Hadhari* or "civilization Islam" which had become the hallmark of his administration. Abdullah in his talks with the Prime Minister, Manmohan Singh stressed that Malaysia was India's largest trade partner in ASEAN and went to sign three agreements one between Antrix Corporation Ltd., commercial arm of the Indian Space Research Organisation, and the Measat Global to pool their satellite capacities, a letter of intent between Antrix and Measat on procurement of Measat-4 satellite and an agreement for construction of a new international airport in Hyderabad.[116] Twelve more memoranda of understanding were signed separately between Indian and Malaysian companies at the business forum addressed by Mr. Badawi during his visit. These included agreements in railways, information technology and biotechnology.

In recent years, Malaysia's investments in India through its national oil corporation Petronas (which is listed in Fortune 500) may already exceed Indian participation in the Malaysian economy. For example, Petronas subsidiary, Mitco Labuan invested some US$1.37 billion in

---

[115] According to the Centre for Independent Journalism (www.cijmalaysia.org), the deputy minister's remarks were reported in *Malay Mail* and night editions of Chinese newspapers *Nanyang Siang Pau, China Press, Guang Ming Daily* and *Sin Chew Daily*.

[116] The consortium of GMR Infrastructure Limited and Malaysia Airports Holdings Berhad has been selected by the Andhra Pradesh and Central Governments following a competitive bidding process to develop a Greenfield international airport through public private partnership at Shamshabad near Hyderabad, about 20 km from the existing airport at Begumpet. *The Hindu,* December 21, 2004.

India in 2005 and has joint ventures with Indian companies engaged in importing, exporting, bottling, storage, marketing and distribution of LPG in bulk. Petronas has also plans to set up petrol pumps throughout India.[117]

Pointing to the many similarities between India and Malaysia, he stressed, "[L]ike India, Malaysia is striving to sustain massive economic growth in order to ensure social justice. Like you, we want all our people to benefit from sustained economic growth. Like you, we don't want to leave behind a single citizen because of a lack of opportunity for education and employment. And like you, we want to make an impact internationally at this time of rapid globalisation".[118] Malaysia, he underlined, was keen to invest more to strengthen India's infrastructure and referred to the statement from New Delhi that half a trillion dollars' worth investment would be required in the next few years.

We will now turn to some hard statistics on trade and investment to get better picture of the actual character of Malaysia's relations with China and India and to make some informed comparisons.

In 2005 and 2006, Malaysia's major trading partners, ranked in order of the volume of exports were: ASEAN, USA, EU, China and Hong Kong, Japan, South Korea and Taiwan. Singapore took the lion's share of ASEAN's exports with 59 percent in 2006 but is ranked second to USA, with 19 percent, followed by EU, 13 percent, Japan, 9 percent, China and Hong Kong, 12 percent, South Korea, 4 percent and Taiwan, 3 percent.[119] This pattern of trade has not changed appreciably since the mid-1970s. Perhaps only the emergence of China as the fourth largest major trading partner and the inclusion of the UK within the EU are the major changes. The US is now Malaysia's

---

[117] See http://economictimes.indiatimes.com/articleshow/401921.cms and http://www.financialexpress.com/news/petronas-lines-up-rs-25k-cr-for-oil-retail-in-india/215328/ (accessed 20 Oct 08).

[118] As cited in *The Hindu*, December 21, 2004.

[119] Figures are rounded. Figures are also drawn from the *Economic Report 2007/2008*.

largest trading partner with 14 percent of total trade Electronic and Electrical (E&E) products accounting for 77.5 percent of exports. Japan's share, at number three, has also declined considerably while USA's share has risen sharply. China's rise is also to be noted as perhaps the most significant development in the 2000s. In one year (2005–06), Malaysia's exports to China increased by 21 percent. Rapid developments in China's ICT sector have fueled demand for E&E products from Malaysia. India, which in the past did not feature prominently in Malaysia's overall trade, has become an important export market with about 3 percent of exports. As for foreign direct investment main sources of FDI (2006) in Malaysia were Japan, Netherlands, Australia, USA, and Singapore. China and India still do not feature prominently as shown in the table below.

Sources of Foreign Investment in Approved Projects in Malaysia (2002–2006), Selected Countries

Country	Foreign Investment (RM)
USA	13,540,033,142
Japan	10,977,141,943
Germany	10,569,397,825
Singapore	8,564,122,206
India	925,544,907
China	663,236,723

Source: Malaysian Industrial Development Authority.

The brief reality check using hard economic data on trade and investment show that while China and India have become somewhat significant to Malaysia's economic well-being, the US, Japan and European countries still remain of paramount significance. Singapore at this juncture figures not only prominently in trade but also in foreign direct investment. A deeper analysis of the character of foreign direct investment would show the electronic and electrical (E&E) industry remains the mainstay of the Malaysian manufacturing sector and that the major investors are the countries mentioned above. Having said this, in more recent years, Malaysia has clearly raised the profile of relations with both China and India as we have indicated in this chapter.[120]

Turning to another areas of economic activity, there has been an increasing interest in Islamic banking in Malaysia since the 1908s which saw this banking sector expand to RM143.7 billion by the end of 2006, accounting for 12.1 percent of total banking assets.[121] As of July 2007, there were 11 Islamic banks and subsidiaries in the country. Malaysia, using its Muslim credentials, has also tried to turn itself into a hub for trading in *halal* products and services. A political economy perspective would suggest that a policy of diversifying and leveraging economic partnerships has been an important strategy for Malaysia. It would seem that economic partnerships with China and India are part of such a strategy.

Concluding Remarks

Asia's political and economic ascendancy suggests that Malaysia should reconfigure its overall positioning, postures, strategies and policies to accommodate the new reality for its own benefit and advantage. An empirical rendering of Malaysia relations with China and India over the last five decades or so reveals that foreign policy has indeed been periodically adjusted to suit the political winds as well as the changing economic dynamics of the times. Malaysia's policy of Western alignment during the height of the Cold War shifted palpably to one of non-alignment for which the diplomatic recognition of China in 1974 proved crucial. Balancing between the more traditional and more cooperative ties with India and the more fractious relations with China proved to be important from the 1980s through till the 1990s. It would also be fair to say that Malaysia to some extent bandwagoned on the rise of East Asia by the end of the 1990s. Malaysia's high profile pre-

---

[120] Malaysian overtures to India have been quite prominent in the 2000s; a trade promotional event dubbed "Incredible India" was held in December 2003, and a conference, "India — The Emerging Economic Giant" was held in Kuala Lumpur in January 2005.

[121] Figures are from *Economic Report, 2007/2008*.

mier Mahathir Mohamad openly argued for the establishment of an East Asian grouping to the exclusion of "Western" countries like Australia and New Zealand and at different times chose to snub both the Commonwealth and APEC.

However, the early infatuation with a Japan-centric East Asian ascendancy has given way to the more measured ASEAN-sponsored notion of the ASEAN Plus Three and the East Asian Summit in the post-Mahathir period. Economic development is seen to now be tied in with a more comprehensive globalization process which would entail Malaysia balancing its interests vis-à-vis all major players, be they East Asian, South Asian, European or North American. It is clear that this approach will now provide the overall thrust of policy for Malaysia along with a political economy approach that will hedge its increasing stake in Asia and the Muslim World with an economic dependence and continued partnership with the US and Europe.

Chapter 6

A Japanese Perspective on the Rise of China and India: Opportunities, Concerns, and Potential Threats[122]

Minoru Koide

Introduction

In principle, Japan welcomes the recent rise of China and India. The development of the two countries offers expanded economic opportunities for Japanese trade and investments. Their increasing commitments to multilateralism promote institution building in East Asia, which has been a long strategic goal for Japan. The inclusion of India in multilateral political process in East Asia is in turn expected to provide a buffer between China and Japan, the two countries traditionally competing for the leadership role in the region.

At the same time, however, Japan is concerned about the relative decline of its importance as China and India emerge as major powers in

---

[122] The original version of this paper was prepared for Mahatma Gandhi–Daisaku Ikeda Peace Research Conference on *"The Rise of China and India: Towards a Harmonious Region?"* organised by the East Asian Institute, Singapore, sponsored by Lam Kin-Chung Morning Sun Charity Fund and Dr Ho Hau-Wong, Thursday on 21 August 2008, at Hotel Park Royal on Beach Road, Singapore.

East Asia and the world. Environmental degradation associated with the development of China, and to a lesser extent with that of India, increasingly brings economic and health problems to the Japanese society. Japan is also worried about the possibility of domestic turmoil in China and India, where the rapid economic developments are respectively widening a socio-economic gap between the rich and the poor.

At least potentially, Japan recognizes that the rise of China and India is a threat for its interests. Both China and India developed nuclear weapons but they refused to join the nuclear non-proliferation treaty. As the sole country that ever experienced the real cruelty of nuclear weapons, Japan sees any moves to weaken the NPT system with utmost sensitivity. The Sino–US rivalry as a result of the increasing Chinese national power is also a potential threat for Japan because the security and prosperity of Japan depends on the United States and China. The Japanese Ministry of Defense, emphasizes a threat in the emerging military cooperation among Russia, China, and India, although the Japanese Ministry of Foreign Affairs does not necessarily share such a view.

Enhanced Economic Chances

The recent rise of China and India has enhanced economic opportunities for Japan as well as many other countries in East Asia. By 2000, the United States was the largest trade partner of Japan, amounting to 29.7% of its export and 19.0% of its import. Since 2004, however, China has been the biggest trade partner of Japan. In 2007, mainland China alone, i.e. except Hong Kong, amounted of 20.6% of Japanese import and 15.3% of Japanese export while that of US amounted to 11.4% and 20.1% respectively. Mainland China alone was still the second largest export partner of Japan. If Hong Kong' share (5.5%) is included in this statistics, China becomes the largest export market for Japan. Japanese direct investment in China expanded rapidly since 2001 when China joined World Trade Organization (WTO). In 2005, Japan recorded 3,269 investment projects with US$653 million value, more than doubling its investment in China in 2001.[123] Though Japanese investment in China has been showing some downturn fluctuations since 2006, Japan is still competing with South Korea to be the largest investment country for China.[124] On the whole, by stimulating rapid economic growth in its surrounding regions and countries, the economic rise of China is fast replacing United States and that of East Asia in Japanese economic relations.

Compared to the real impacts of the economic rise of China on Japan, the rise of India has yet to provide real changes beyond symbolic expectations. Despite the fact that India recorded 6.6% economic growth in average in the 1990s, and even faster development since the beginning of this century, Indian shares in Japanese trade have stayed relatively the same throughout the period, amounting to 0.9% of Japanese export and 0.7% of Japanese import respectively in 2007. Between 1991–2006, the accumulated value of Japanese investments in India amounted to 3.2 billion dollar, much less than 4.6 billion dollar Japanese investments in China in the year 2006 alone.[125] In the India–Japan Study Group Report issued in June 2006, the officials and scholars of both the countries agreed that the economic relations between India–Japan have not fully realized their potentially expected levels. Emphasizing the commensurability of the two economies as well as the recent rapid growth of IT industry in India, the Study Group Report expects the expansion of trade and investment, the promotion of technology transfer, and the mutual understanding of different business cultures between India and Japan.[126]

---

[123] The statistic figures of the Japanese trade and investment are available in the JETRO website. Available at http://www.jetro.go.jp. For the Japanese investment in China in particular, see http://www.jetro.go.jp/world/asia/cn/stat_06/.

[124] If regions are included, Hong Kong and the Virgin Islands surpassed Japan in terms of the value of investment in China.

[125] The total accumulated value of Japanese investments in China between 1991 and 2007 almost reached 59 billion US dollars according to the Commercial Department of China. See http://www.21ccs.jp/china_performance/performance2007_01.html .

[126] Available at http://www.mofa.go.jp/region/asia-paci/india/report0606.pdf.

The primary reason why the trade between Japan and India stays at a relatively low level compared to their respective economic sizes is that China and Southeast Asian countries compete with India in their trade with Japan. Although India recently increased its exports in the areas of textile manufacturing and IT software, China and Southeast Asian countries prevent these exports to Japan by expanding proportionally to the growth of its overall economy. Moreover, in the field of human and cultural exchange, which is expected to provide the foundation of the large scale economic transactions, India is far behind China and even Southeast Asia.[127]

Since diversification of trade partners and structures were important to both Japan and India, the political leaders of both countries agreed to expand bilateral trade and other economic relations. In August 2007, when the Japanese Prime Minister Abe visited India, he and the Indian Prime Minister Man Mohan Singh issued a joint statement to double the amount of the annual bilateral trade up to US 20 billion dollars by 2010.[128] The two leaders also agreed to start a bilateral negotiation between the two countries on the Economic Partnership Agreement as soon as possible. Prime Minister Singh reciprocated Abe's visit by visiting Japan twice in 2008, first in July 2008 when the G8 summit meeting was held in Hokkaido Japan, and again in October for the Japanese–Indian summit meeting. During his October visit, Singh expressed his satisfaction regarding the progress of the bilateral economic relations toward the goals agreed one year before.[129]

---

[127] The Japanese–Indian Common Study report (June 2006) points to the fact that in the year 2004 the number of Indian students studying in Japan was 410 whereas that of Chinese students was 80592. See http://www.meti.go.jp/policy/trade_policy/epa/data/jinEPA_report_j.pdf.

[128] Clause 10 of the Joint Statement on the Roadmap for New Dimensions to the Strategic and Global Partnership between Japan and India (hereafter the Joint Statement on the Roadmap), issued in New Delhi on August 22, 2007. See http://www.mofa.go.jp/region/asia-paci/pmv0708/joint-2.html.

[129] Available at http://www.mofa.go.jp/region/asia-paci/india/pmv0810/joint_s.html

Development of Multilateral Institutions and Frameworks in East Asia

After the devastating end of the Pacific War, Japan adopted the constitution renouncing the war, and introduced as its diplomacy guideline the so-called Yoshida doctrine to concentrate on economic development while limiting its commitment to security issues. The outbreak of the Cold War, however, forced Japan to introduce the Self Defense Forces under its peace constitution. The contradiction between the reality of world politics and the ideals of its constitution divided the Japanese domestic politics, culminating in violence over the amendment of the US–Japanese Security Treaty in 1960. Since then the argument of national strategy was long regarded as too sensitive in the Japanese domestic politics.

One of the rare strategic goals that could expect broad national support was the promotion of Japanese ties with its Asian neighbors. For conservatives represented by the Liberal Democratic Party, better relations with Asian countries were regarded as expansion of Japanese economic opportunities. For those who supported the Socialist Party, which dogmatically interpreted and supported the Article Nine of the Japanese constitution, improved relations with Asian neighbors were welcomed as an effort for reconciliation after Japanese aggressions committed before 1945.[130]

During the later half of the 1960s, the Japanese government began to consider the idea of free trade area in Asia. However, it was concerned that Japanese interest in the regional framework would be regarded by its Asian neighbors as a revival of its ambitious

---

[130] Most Asian countries directly opposed to, or at least officially reserved the ratification of the San Francisco Peace Treaty with Japan. Both China and India strongly opposed the treaty. See Kent Calder, Higashi Ajianiokeru Chiikishugi to Doumei (Regionalism and Alliance in East Asia), Chapter 4 in *Tokai Daigaku Heiwa Senryaku* Kokusai Kenkyujo *ed. Higashi Ajia ni Kyodotai ha Dekiruka* (Is it possible to establish a community in East Asia?) Shakaihyoronsha, 2006, p. 82.

"the Greater East Asian Co-prosperity Sphere" scheme. Therefore the country strictly limited its argument to the economic regional framework. Moreover, Japan tried to promote discussions on the regional framework often through non-official channels in which Japanese officials participated in their "private" capacity. Furthermore, Japan always emphasized US participation as a necessary condition for the introduction of its projected regional framework. In so doing, Japan tried to demonstrate both to its Asian neighbors and the United States that its projection of the regional economic framework was not an attempt to pursue Japanese leadership role in the region.[131]

The first Asia Pacific Economic Cooperation (APEC) ministerial meeting in 1989 realized the Japanese long time diplomatic dream. In the negotiation process toward the first APEC meeting, Japan requested the participation of ASEAN and the US in the new institution. On the other hand, in late 1992 when the then Malaysian Prime Minister Mahathir proposed the formation of an East Asian Group without the US in order to overcome the US–EU stalemate in the GATT Uruguay Round negotiations, Japan did not support Mahathir's idea. At that time, Washington also rejected any attempts to exclude the US from groupings in East Asia and the Pacific.

The 1997 Asian financial crisis was the turning point for the development of regional framework in East Asia and the Pacific. Although Washington rejected the Japanese proposal to introduce Asian Monetary Fund while insisting the application of IMF conditionality to the crisis situations of Asian countries, it did not oppose the gathering of leaders of Japan, China, South Korea, and ASEAN countries to deal with the financial crisis. After the 1997 meeting, which was the *de faco* realization of Mahathir's proposal in the early 1990s, the regional framework in Asia increasingly shifted its focus to East Asia from the Pacific.[132]

---

[131] Minoru Koide, The East Asian Community An Unattainable Dream? *Sodai Heiwa Kenkyu* (Soka University Peace Research) Vols. 22 & 23 (March 2002), pp. 69–81.

[132] Minoru Koid, Whither Our Region? A Comparative Analysis on the Asia Pacific and East Asia, *Sodai Heiwa Kenkyu*. Special Issue on the East Asian Community, March 2005, pp. 59–74.

The recent rise of China and India has provided further momentum for institution building process in East Asia. Under Koizumi's administration, the Japanese government adopted the idea of the "East Asian Community" as its grand strategy for its Asian policy. Therefore, increasing interests of China and India in multilateral institutions in East Asia have been welcomed by Japan.[133]

Traditionally, China emphasized bilateral diplomacy rather than multilateral dealings except for propagating the rather ideological three-world strategy under Mao's reign.[134] Ever since the 1997 Asian financial crisis, China began to focus more on the regional cooperation mechanism with its neighbors. The establishment of Shanghai Cooperation Organization in 2001, the beginning of FTA negotiations with ASEAN countries, the participation in the Treaty of Amity and Cooperation in Southeast Asia (TAC), and the organization of Six-Party talks on the North Korean nuclear issue all indicate the shift in Chinese foreign policy toward multilateralism.[135]

Specifically since 2004, as Japan did under Koizumi, China also adopted the idea of the East Asian Community as its diplomatic strategy. Although Sino–Japanese relations experienced many difficulties as Koizumi visited the Yasukuni Shrine repeatedly during his terms, China in fact shares many ideas with Japan regarding the East Asian community as a policy goal. In pursuit of multilateralism in East Asia, China tries to: (1) put primary emphasis on economic cooperation

---

[133] Nishiguchi Kiyoshi ed. *Higashi Ajia Kyodotai no Kouchiku* (The Building of the East Asian Community). Tokyo: Mineruba Shobo, 2006, pp. 6–12 & 33–38.

[134] Former Chairperson of Chinese Communist Party Mao Zedong developed the Three Worlds Theory to justify and emphasize the Chinese leadership role in the non alignment movement in the 1960s and 1970s. According to Mao, the world was divided into the First World consisting of the two superpowers (i.e. the United States and the Soviet Union) at that time, the Second World of rich allies of the superpowers, and the Third World of all the other developing countries. See King C. Chen (ed.), *China and the Three Worlds*, New York, M E Sharpe Inc, 1978.

[135] Sato Toyoshi (ed). *Higashi Ajia Kyodotai no Kanousei: Nicchu Kankei no Saikento* (The Possibility of the East Asian Community: The Re-examination of the Sino-Japanese Relations), Tokyo, Ochanomizu Shobo, 2006, pp. 333–338.

rather than attempting a radical change in security systems in the region, (2) to support the ASEAN leadership in region building efforts, and (3) to keep the US leadership role and function in the region while promoting "open regionalism" as a political slogan for East Asia.

In order to maintain stable international environments favorable for its rapid economic development, India has also increased its commitments in the process of regional institution building in East Asia. Since its adoption of "Look East Policy" in the mid 1990s, India actively engaged in economic talks and cooperation with ASEAN countries and improved its relations with China.[136] India and Japan have been continuing the mutual visits by respective top leaders almost every year, which resulted in the agreements of India–Japan Partnership in 2000, 2005, and 2007. Although there are arguments against the feasibility of including India as a member of East Asia,[137] India successfully joined the East Asian summit in late 2005 and the Indian participation was welcomed by Japan.

After US Hegemony? A Balancer Role Between China and India

In the process of multilateral institution building in East Asia, Japan has cautiously avoided giving an impression that such a move is seen as an attempt to exclude or replace US leadership role in the region. After experiencing almost hysteric US reactions in the 1990s against any moves that may even slightly lead to the exclusion of the US from an East Asian group, Japan repeatedly confirmed its commitment to the US-centered order in Asia. However, increased economic interdependence and cooperation among Asian countries since the 1997 Asian Financial crisis, and the continued development of China and India as well as other economies in the region, promoted the emergence of an Asian group. As the formation of the Asian group becomes an undeniable

---

[136] Tanaka Akihiko, *Ajia no Nakano Nippon* (Japan in Asia), Tokyo, NTT Shuppan, 2007, p. 232.

[137] Hiratsuka Daisuke, *Higashi Ajia no Chosen* (The Challenge of East Asia), Tokyo: Ajia Keizai Kenkyujo, 2006, pp. 8–9.

fact rather than a political slogan, the US government cautiously changed its attitude towards multilateral institutions in East Asia.[138]

If the rise of China is an irreversible process in the 21st century world politics, it would be indeed much more rational to prepare for it rather than to resist it. Japan, like most other countries in Asia, should be prepared for the post-US hegemony order in the region. In this context, Japan needs to welcome the rise of India and China for various reasons. First, the emergence of India (and probably South Korea) as a major power in East Asia is expected to reduce tensions regarding the leadership role between China and Japan in the region. Although it is often argued that the power of China will overwhelm that of Japan in all terms by the turn of this century, Japanese economic power is still much larger than that of China today. Therefore, whether they may like it or not, China and Japan will soon have to go through a difficult process in which the power balance between the two countries is shifted from the one side to the other. As China and Japan traditionally compete for the hegemony in East Asia, the issue of leadership should be treated with utmost sensitivity. As India and South Korea become major players in East Asian politics, the issue of leadership will be of concern to China and Japan.[139]

Second, the rise of India is expected to contribute to the introduction of a more favorable regional order for Japan than the China-centered one. Japan often describes the importance of India as the world's largest democratic country that shares basic values with Japan such as the rule of law. Among its immediate geographical neighbors, Japan has no partner sharing the long tradition of liberal democracy. As Japan tries to promote multilateral orders in East Asia along with its esteemed political values, the participation of India in the East Asian international orders has a strategic significance for Japan.[140]

---

[138] Mike Mochizuki, U.S.–Japan Relations in the Asia-Pacific Region, Chapter 1 in Akira Iriye & Robert A. Wampler (eds.), *Partnership: the United States and Japan 1951–2001*, Tokyo: Kodansha International, 2001, pp. 29–31.

[139] Lim Wha Shin, Higashi Ajia Keizaiken no Kosatsu (An Analysis on the East Asian Economic Zone), in *Higashi Ajia ni Kyodotai ha Dekiruka*, p. 138.

[140] The Japanese-Indian Common Study report (June 2006). Available at http://www.meti.go.jp/policy/trade_policy/epa/data/jinEPA_report_j.pdf.

Third, conventional wisdom of diplomacy tells that, in the competition between the two powers, the third party can enjoy wider room of maneuverability. This does not mean that Japan will try to play a balancing role between China and India in the process of institution building in East Asia. However, if Japan tries to have an influence vis-a-vis the two nuclear powers, its position in the Sino-Indian rivalry will be an important resource tip for its diplomacy.

Three Concerns

Japan passing or nothing

Japan is concerned about the possibility that the rise of China and India may result in the relatively less important role of Japan in the world political and economic order. Both China and India still have huge margins of quantitative development because of their large sizes with respect to population and land. As of 2005, GDP of Japan was about twice as much as that of China and almost six times larger than that of India. However, if the wide gap between economic growth rates of China and India vis-à-vis Japan is to continues, it is possible that Japan will be on per with China around the year 2020. It will take longer for India to surpass Japan, but there is no reason to deny the possibility that India can follow the same path as China. In addition to economic resources such as large population and land, both China and India possess cultural resources which originate from their long history as ancient empires. As a former British colony, India is comprised of a large English-speaking population which is a clear advantage in today's globalizing world.[141]

In addition to its relative position to rising China and India, Japan is more concerned about US changing attitude towards the country. However, no bilateral alliance can be eternal in changing international relations. In reality, the US–Japan security alliance has not been free

---

[141] Joseph S. Nye, Jr., *Soft Power: The Means to Success in World Politics*, New York: Public Affairs, 2004, translated by Yamaoka Yoichi as *Sofuto Pawa*, Tokyo: Nihonkeizai Shimbunsha, 2004, pp. 142–144.

from changes because it is not a symmetrically designed system. Under the US–Japan Security Treaty, the United States promises to defend the Japanese territory while Japan promises to reciprocate by permitting the US military bases in its territory. Such an asymmetrical characteristic in the bilateral system has been a source of frustration for both sides. From the US perspective, Japan is regarded as a free rider on the US security efforts. From the Japanese perspective, a nationalistically critical nationalistic voice has been raised within domestic politics which argues that the perpetual stationing of foreign military in its territory is a humiliating arrangement not worthy of an independent state. Such nationalistic sentiments are periodically inflamed when crimes against Japanese women by the US servicemen stationed in Japan are reported by the media.

The possibility of the US discarding its alliance with Japan might be discussed either in Japan or in the United States. The abolition of the US–Japan alliance is unimaginable for Japan. However, the texts of the treaty that supports the bilateral alliance system says that "either Party may give notice to the other Party of its intention to terminate the Treaty, in which case the Treaty shall terminate one year after such notice has been given".[142] The termination of the treaty does not require an agreement between the United States and Japan. Therefore, at least in principle, it should be noted that the US–Japan alliance system can be discarded through a simple procedure although the Japanese Ministry of Foreign Affairs emphasizes that Article 10 ensures the automatic extension of the treaty unless either party shows explicit intensions of abrogating it.[143]

However, the United States can review the meaning and role of the US–Japan Security Treaty System when it accepts multipolar/regional orders in Asia where major roles are played by China and India. Therefore, there is a possibility of the US reviewing the meaning of the US–Japan Security Treaty system in the near future. The multilateral

---

[142] Article 10 of the US–Japan Security Treaty.

[143] See the analysis of major articles of the US–Japan Security Treaty by the Japanese Ministry of Foreign Affairs. Available at http://www.mofa.go.jp/Mofaj/area/usa/hosho/jyoyaku_k.html.

security organization in East Asia seems a remote dream because of the differences in political values and development levels among the regional states. It is to be noted that the corruption of the Cold War system occurred within such a short period that only few specialists could expect it occur.

Given the prospect of multi-polarity in East Asia as a result of the rise of China and India, not only the United States but also Japan may began to explore a possible alternative to the US–Japan alliance. Regarding its alliance policy, Japan already experienced the least expected events. At the Washington conference in 1921–22, the Anglo–Japanese Alliance Treaty was unexpectedly discarded. The termination of the bilateral treaty, which had been called the back bone of the Japanese diplomacy then, left Japan anxious of its future security even though the Washington Conference itself recognized the expansion of Japanese interests in the post World War I order in East Asia. This forced Japan to pursue its adventurous military expansion in China after the Washington Treaty system experience which finally led it to the devastating war with the United States.[144] This historical experience implies that an unquestioned reliance on the bilateral security system is not advisable for the Japanese diplomacy. There is no reason to believe that Japan has learned anything from this lesson.

Environmental burdens

The rise of China and India has resulted in environmental concerns not only in Japan but also in the Asian region. Indeed, the recent economic development of the two large countries has rapidly increased the consumption of energy resources, accelerating the degradation of natural environments, and producing ever increasing CO_2 emissions. It remains to be seen whether planet earth can withstand the development of the two population giants to the level of today's Western Europe, North America, or Japan. As of 2002, China accounted to 14.5% of the world's

---

[144] Minoru Koide, Nichi Ei Domei Shuryo Katei no Kenkyu (An Analysis on the Termination Process of the Anglo-Japanese Alliance), the Memorial Journal of the 25th Anniversary of Soka University (December 1995), pp. 1224–1232.

total CO_2 emissions of 24.1 billion tons and while India and Japan accounted to 4.4% and 4.9% respectively.[145] As China and India maintain higher economic growth rates than Japan, the assumption is that the two countries will emit more CO_2 gases than Japan, even though their economies still seem to have much room for expansion respectively.

In addition to environmental concerns at the global level, Japan, being an immediate neighbor of China, is more concerned about the environmental influences of Chinese economic development over its territory. The expansion of desert area in China has already resulted in the spreading yellow sand to the western part of Japan early spring every year. In addition to Japan, the yellow sand also spreads to Mongolia and South Korea, causing enormous economic losses and health damages in these countries. In order to survey and analyze the situation of the yellow sand, governments of Japan, South Korea, Mongolia and China thought of using international networks to collect meteorological data. However, in March 2008, China decided not to support the international efforts saying that information about the national weather is confidential data related to national security.[146]

Instances like this result in Japan becoming anxious about importing food products from China because Japan gets 60% of its food supply from foreign countries and much of this comes from China.[147] Recent instances of polluted food have affected credibility of Chinese products in Japan. In October 2008, the Japanese Ministries of Agriculture, Forestry, and Fishery organized campaign headquarters called "Food Action Nippon Movement," the primarily goal of which is to raise the Japanese self-food-supply ratio from current 40% to 45% in seven years.[148] Although this movement is not necessarily regarded as an

---

[145] Ando Hiroshi, EANET: Higashi Ajia no Senkuteki Rentai (EANET: A Leading Example of Regional Cooperation toward the East Asian Community), in *Higashi Ajia ni Kyodotai ha Dekiruka*, p. 185.

[146] China's Yellow Sand Hits Japan and South Korea, AFP, March 3, 2008. Avilable at http://dsc.discovery.com/news/2008/03/03/japan-desert-sand.html

[147] Avilable at http://www.maff.go.jp/j/zyukyu/zikyu_ritu/011.html.

[148] Avilable at http://www.maff.go.jp/j/press/kanbo/anpo/081007.html.

action targeting Chinese products, the Japanese effort to increase domestic food supply will in the long run affect the structure and procedures of Sino–Japanese trade.

Political instability as a result of widening economic gap

Rapid economic growth is often accompanied by the widening gap of incomes and life conditions in a domestic society. Unfortunately, China and India are no exceptions to this. Moreover, the recent increase in international food and energy prices hit the poor more severely everywhere in the world. The recent globalization of the world economy has resulted in changing traditional life styles and societies. In such a sceneries some religious and nationalistic groups resort to extreme actions like terrorism to express their frustration against socio-economic disadvantages, which they assume are imposed by developed countries. Since both China and India have seen ethnic conflicts and independent movements in their respective domestic societies, there are always concerned about the political instability that might be caused by disadvantaged minorities.

Because of its dependence on the Chinese market as well as its geographical proximity, Japan has been always paying attention to the possibility of domestic political turmoil in China. In their response to these Japanese concerns, Chinese intellectuals by and large express optimistic views that though there have been concerns about political conflicts and turmoil since the beginning of the reform and open door policy of the Chinese economy in the late 1970s, the rapid development of China has been unstoppable in the last three decades.

Interestingly, predictions by intellectuals occur suddenly and there are ample of instances of such occurrences in the history. For instance, international recognition of human rights issues arouse international interest, in domestic issues — Chinese administration of Tibet continues to be a source of internationally recognized political instability. As for the Tibet issue, the Japanese government has not regarded it as an international concern as many Western states do. However, as the outright violation of human rights or the severe persecution of national movements are reported in the western media, Japan might have to rethink about its response to this issue.

The potential political turmoil in India is also a big concern for Japan because the security of sea lanes through which oil imports reach Japan from the Middle East along the Indian Ocean would be affected.[149] Moreover, there is an increase in the number of pirate incidences in these sea lanes. In order to secure its vital trade route, Japan needs to continuously support the Indian government in enhancing the security sea lanes along the India Ocean. The Joint Statement issued during Abe's visit to India in August 2007 confirmed the intention to enhance cooperation in maritime safety, maritime security and protection of marine environment through combined exercises, regular meetings of heads of the two Coast Guards, and cooperation based on the Memorandum on Cooperation signed between the two Coast Guards.[150]

Three Threats

NPT dominos

As a country that has experienced the real catastrophe and disaster of nuclear weapons, Japan always views nuclear issues with utmost sensitivity. The development of nuclear weapons by China in the 1960s and by India in the 1990s has triggered strong criticism in Japan. As a non-nuclear member, Japan regards the possible corruption of NPT systems as a very serious threat to its national security. In this context, Japan regards China and India as countries that destabilize NPT systems. Whenever Japanese official papers are issued about the current situation of NPT systems, they emphasize that India, along with Pakistan, did not join the 1995 UN-adopted CTBT treaty while China signed, but

---

[149] China also depends on the security of the Indian Ocean through which 80% of its imported oil from the Middle East reaches the country. Fujimaki Yuichi, "Higashi Ajia ni Okeru Enerugi Anzenhosho (Energy Security in East Asia), in *Higashi Ajia ni Kyodotai ha Dekiruka,* p. 171.

[150] Clause 9 of the Joint Statement on the Roadmap. Avilable at http://www.mofa.go.jp/region/asia-paci/pmv0708/joint-2.html.

has yet to ratify it.[151] In the wake of recent Six-Party talks on the North Korean nuclear issues, Japan is cautiously evaluating the Chinese commitment to nuclear non-proliferation efforts in Asia.

The Japanese public school education has made students aware of the cruelty and misery caused by Hiroshima and Nagasaki experiences. This has resulted in anti-nuclear sentiments being deeply rooted among the Japanese. Therefore, the fact that Japanese security is actually protected by the US nuclear umbrella, does not necessarily change their opinion of nuclear weapons. Although the possibility of nuclear Japan has been sporadically argued in Washington DC, that scenario sounds quite unrealistic to anybody with a slightest understanding of Japanese domestic politics and sentiments.

The Japanese anti-nuclear sentiments are so strong that, once initiated, the US nuclear forces that actually defend the Japanese security might be targeted. Japan was therefore, shocked when the Bush administration offered nuclear technology to India in 2006 despite India opposing the NPT treaty. Most Japanese newspapers criticized the US decision that would shake the NPT system. The Japanese government, however, was not very critical of this, though the Japanese media covered the event extensively. Probably, considering the strategic implications of its relations with the United States and India, the Japanese government tried to avoid initiating anti-nuclear sentiments among the Japanese.

Although the Japanese commitment to the NPT system is strong, should circumstances force Japan to withdraw from NPT, it is likely that NPT comes to an end. Therefore, any actions to shake the Japanese commitment to NPT systems by China and India should be regarded as potential threats not only to Japan but also to the world as a whole.

Sino–US rivalry

If the NPT dominos, however serious their results may be, are still hypothetical, the escalation of Sino–US rivalry may pose as a worst

---

[151] Abe Junichi, *Chuugoku to Higashi Ajia no Anzenhosho* (China and Security in East Asia), Tokyo, Meitoku Shuppansha, 2006, pp. 192–194.

scenario for Japan. First, the Sino–US rivalry might land Japan in a serious dilemma because Japan depends on the US for security issues and on China for economy-related aspects. Second, the excessive Sino–US rivalry destabilizes regional orders in East Asia. The Sino–US tensions over the Taiwan straits may pose an immediate threat to the Japanese territory. If confronted with such a situation, Japan may have to focus on contradicting relations between the Japanese constitution and the US–Japan Security system, which have been intentionally left vague, due to serious collisions in the Japanese domestic politics.

As seen in the Beijing Olympic Games, the increasing national power of China is associated with stronger national pride among the Chinese public. The stronger national pride may in turn lead to the stronger claim over the issue of Taiwan, making the compromise between China and the United States more difficult. Those who are familiar with the current situation of the Two Shore relations tend to deny the likelihood of such a scenario by quoting that the *de facto* economic integration between mainland China and Taiwan is already so deep to make any serious military crises over the Taiwan straits impossible.

Russo–Chinese–Indian military triangle

Japan perceives the Russo–Chinese–Indian military triangle as a potential threat. The 2006 Defense White Paper of Japan covers five pages describing the Russian military cooperation with China and India.[152] Both China and India have respectively engaged in security talks and cooperation with Japan in recent years. Therefore, the development of Russo–Chinese–India military cooperation should not be regarded as a threat to Japan. Instead, the trilateral security cooperation should be viewed as a natural development of multilateral diplomatic efforts by the three countries.

---

[152] The Japan Defense Agency (ed.), Higashi Ajia Senryaku Gaikan 2006 (The Survey of the Strategic Situation in East Asia 2006), pp. 186–190.

However, Japan is concerned about the fact that the recent economic rise of China and India has led to the steady expansion of military power of the two countries. In terms of purchasing power, Chinese and Indian military expenditures were ranked the second and the third respectively in the year 2002, next only to United States. Between 1998 and 2002, China was the largest importer of conventional weapons, India stood third (where Taiwan stood at the second position). It is also noted that the recent improvement of Sino–Indian relations promoted bilateral cooperation in acquisition efforts of third world oil assets.[153]

In the case of China, Japan is concerned of not only with the PRC's increasing military expenditure, but also its continued lack of transparency. Moreover, the Japanese government is cautiously watching every Chinese attempt to extend its sovereignty over the disputed islands with Japan.[154] The Chinese attempt to drill in the potentially oil-rich disputed area in turn stimulates Japanese nationalism. Therefore, any signs of closeness between China and Russia, which also has a long dispute with Japan over the Northern Territory, is perceived as a potential threat to the Japanese territorial integrity.

Geographically located far from Japan, India does not pose a threat to Japanese territory as China does. However, through the escalation of the India–Pakistani nuclear development competition, India might threaten the existence of NPT system which Japan regards as its vital diplomatic goal. The rise of energy-rich Russia, which faces similar ethnic tensions to that of China and India, may try to form an anti–US triangle with the two Asian giants that are invariably unhappy with the US intervention in domestic matters.

The fear of the Russo–Chinese–Indian triangle highlighted by the Defense White Paper of Japan, however, should not be considered as the opinion of the Japanese government. In fact, the Japanese government

---

[153] Sasaki Hiroshi (ed.), *Higashi Ajia Kyosei no Joken* (Conditions for Co-prosperity in East Asia) Tokyo: Seshikishobo, 2006, pp. 172–176.

[154] In 1992 China amended its domestic law to explicitly declare its sovereignty over the disputed islands with Japan. Available at http://www.mofa.go.jp/mofaj/gaiko/bluebook/1992/h04-3-1.htm.

has actively sought security dialogues with the three countries. The Japanese Ministry of Foreign Affairs assumes that the recent Chinese approach to Russia and India is a sign of the Chinese attempt to pursue multilateral diplomacy and promote multi-polarity in the world.[155] In order to maintain stable international environments which are considered as a necessary condition for its top priority goal, i.e. continuous development of its domestic economy, China is trying to maintain good relations with major powers like the US, EU, and Japan. With its neighboring countries, China is trying to promote multilateral diplomacy. Through the Shanghai Cooperative Organization, China is trying to strengthen its relations with Russia and central Asian countries. China is also trying to improve its relations with Southeast Asian countries and India through frameworks like ASEAN and FTAs. These are all concrete examples of the Chinese effort towards multilateral diplomacy.

Conclusion

The recent rise of China and India has resulted in more opportunities than threats for Japan. If Hong Kong is included in its trade statistics, China has already surpassed the United States in terms of being the biggest trade partner for Japan. Japan has always been competing with other Asian neighbors to be the largest investment partner of China. Although it is often said that Japan and India are yet to realize the full potential of their bilateral economic relations, the top leaders of the two countries have repeatedly expressed their commitments to the expansion of the economic relations. Japan is also welcoming the increasing Chinese and Indian involvement in multilateral frameworks in East Asia. The inclusion of the two rising economic powers in the regional framework is expected to promote stability in East Asia. Moreover, the Indian participation in the East Asian political process will provide a buffer between Japan and China which have long been competing for the leadership role in East Asia.

However, the rise of China and India is also a matter of worry to Japan. First, their rise is sometimes interpreted as the relative decline

---

[155] Available at http://www.mofa.go.jp/mofaj/area/china/pdfs/kankei.pdf#01.

of Japan in East Asia. Second, the rapid economic development of the two population giants may cause environmental damage to Japan. Finally, both China and India are experiencing widening gap in their respective society, which may in turn results in domestic political turmoil.

From a different viewpoint, the rise of China and India is regarded as a potential source of threats to Japan. Their continuous rejection of the NPT system is regarded as the biggest source of threat to the Japanese security. As a country that experienced the real damage and cruelty of nuclear attacks, Japan views the development of nuclear weapons by China and India with utmost sensitivity. For a prospective future, Japan will continue to rely on the United States for security issues, and increasingly on the expanding Asian market for its economic prosperity. Therefore, the Sino–US rivalry is another serious source of potential threat to Japan. Military experts in Japan also note the increasing military cooperation among Russia, China, and India as another threat to Japan.

In the long run, the rise of China and India seems to be an irresistible historical trend. As China becomes as powerful a state as the United States, Japan needs to prepare for a difficult adjustment process between the United States and China. Later, India may join that process too, further promoting multi-polar orders in East Asia. Meanwhile, it is projected that Japan, by the year 2050, will have lost one fourth of its current population. To some extent, it seems inevitable that the Japanese relative power and influences in East Asia will decrease while that of China and India will increasingly have larger impacts on the region and the world. Japan should try to promote the formation of an international order based on fundamental values such as basic human rights, democracy, and the rule of law which are practiced by Japan. The rise of China and India indicates that Japan should pursue its soft power rather than its hard power in the 21st century.

Chapter 7

The Rise of China and India: Geo-political Narratives from the Singapore Perspective

Lim Tai Wei

Narratives emanating from Singapore on the rise of China and India tend to emphasize the economic emergence of the two giant economies. Like many other Asia-Pacific countries and, indeed the world, business and commercial analyses of Chinese and Indian economic trends have spawned a massive industry of consulting, news/information, publishing and speaking circuits. But what about geopolitical narratives in international relations, do they also reflect the same levels of optimism, pragmatism, problems and criticisms that economic analyses face? This chapter looks at selected thoughts and individual perceptions of three thinkers who have left their diplomatic/academic footprints on the subject.

Inherent and implicit in any discussion on perspectives, the locality of the analyst or thinker itself becomes a subject of discussion. Singapore-centric perspectives on this subject are not restricted by nationality or citizenship and the three individuals have been chosen based on their Singapore-centric perspectives with their backgrounds straddling diplomacy and academia. Three popular schools of thought can be referenced when it comes to strategic thinking about the rise of

China and India — those of Michael Leifer, Kishore Mahbubani and Tommy Koh. This selection of thinkers is comprehensive or comprehensively representative, rather, based on contributions circulated within the academia, diplomatic circles and by the popular media, generating and contributing to mainstream interest and narratives in Singapore.

One observation that can be made is that there seems to be very few Singapore-centric narratives that are extremely pessimistically critical of the rise of China and India which may be comparable to the likes of Gordon Chang's *The Coming Collapse of China* in the US or rightwing Taiwanese–Japanese Ko Bunyu's highly-racialized *An Introduction to China*. One would also be hard-pressed to find narratives that consider China or India a direct and unequivocal threat to Singapore.

Many factors may account for this. The thoughts of the three individuals may offer some possible explanations for this. Given the internationalist (leading proponent of free economic exchanges) and cosmopolitan background, Singapore has always had a pragmatic policy that worked with all major world powers since independence. In fact, far from being threats, Mahbubani, for example, highlights the positive aspect of China and India's rise to power, citing "China's modernization has already reduced the number of Chinese living in absolute poverty from six hundred million to two hundred million" and "India's growth is also making an equally significant impact".[156]

In a celebratory mood, Mahbubani points out that the reason why United Nations (UN) will "actually meet one of its Millennium Development Goals of reducing global poverty by half by 2015 will be the success of China and India in reducing poverty significantly".[157] This leads to his argument that many Western observers and analysts, including those radically negative ones, fail to "see beyond the lack of a democratic political system" and "miss the massive democratization of the human spirit that is taking place in China" as "hundreds of millions of

---

[156] Kishore Mabhubani, *The New Asian Hemisphere*, New York: Public Affairs, 2008, p. 1.
[157] Kishore Mabhubani, *The New Asian Hemisphere*, New York: Public Affairs, 2008, p. 2.

Chinese who thought they were destined for endless poverty now believe that they can improve their lives through their own efforts".[158]

In terms of internal dynamics, most analyses of Singapore's foreign policy depend on concepts that shore up its natural vulnerabilities such as small state size, the need for survival, realpolitik balance of power pragmatism. Thus, all regional and superpowers are not immediately treated as a threat but as a component of the regional balance of power in Singapore's quest to enhance global and regional interdependence. The emergence of China and India creates a regional superstructure from which Singapore can frame its response and hedge them against more established powers.

Within the region of Southeast Asia, Singapore has an internalized equilibrium in its relations with China or India. Singapore is not located on the peripheries of China (unlike the so-called Greater Chinese societies Taiwan or Hong Kong or sinified outskirts like Vietnam) or India (unlike many Indo–Chinese states). It is located in the center of maritime Southeast Asia where ethnic Chinese who form the majority of Singaporeans (three quarters) are a regional minority treated with caution by neighboring dominant ethnicities. Thus, Singaporeans have treaded carefully, walking a fine line between ethnic identification with their ancestral past and sensitivities towards harmonious relations with indigenous ethnic groups in the region. In other words, mainstream Singapore, its leaders, media and society have been careful in being balanced and measured in their worldviews and conceptualizations of the positions of China, India and Southeast Asia in their lives.

One of Singapore's pillars of foreign policy is its commitment to good relations with its neighbours[159] and the resulting sensitivity to its immediate neighbour's own bilateral relations with China. Regionally, Singapore is sensitive to its neighbours' suspicions of Singapore's Chinese-majority's affiliation with China. Thus, Singapore made it a point to establish formal official diplomatic relations with the People's

---

[158] Kishore Mabhubani, *The New Asian Hemisphere*, New York: Public Affairs, 2008, p. 18.
[159] Tommy Koh , *The Quest for World Order Perspectives of a Pragmatic Idealist*, Singapore, Federal Publications, 1998, p. 178.

Republic of China (3 October 1990) only after Indonesia had done so (8 August 1990). Singapore's sense of its own vulnerabilities imposed a form of self-restraint in its relations with China.

Michael Leifer. The first school of thought in Singapore-centric views of the rise of China and India that is studied in this chapter is the English school of balance of power school led by the highly-respected Michael Leifer, an academic-cum-practitioner in Southeast Asian politics and international relations. Leifer ventures outside academia, personally involved in the creation of Council for Security Cooperation in the Asia–Pacific (CSCAP) and his opinions are often sought after by policy-makers. He has also published more than 20 single-authored and edited and innumerable scholarly articles covering not only the field of international relations of Southeast Asia but also their domestic policies.[160]

Leifer holds up Singapore as the model of a small state utilizing balance of power to overcome its geopolitical vulnerability. Singapore tries to find and employ "a variety of ways of compensating for and reshaping to advantage a regional distribution of power which registers the island the island-state's vulnerability" and this includes engaging in "multilateral forms of cooperative security arrangements" that do not include a military dimension.[161]

Leifer provides an analogy used by a former Foreign Minister of Singapore to describe Singapore's preference for inclusive participation of stakeholders: "When there is a multiplicity of suns, the gravitational pull of each is not only weakened but also by a judicious use of pulls and counter-pulls of gravitational forces, the minor planets have a great freedom of navigation".[162] This was a delicate balance of external interests in which Singapore understood its vulnerabilities and the importance of balancing regional powers and neighbours.

---

[160] Michael Leifer, *Selected Works on Southeast Asia* edited by Chin Kin Wah and Leo Suryadinata Singapore, Institute of Southeast Asian Studies, 2005, p. ix.
[161] Michael Leifer, *Singapore's Foreign Policy*, Great Britain: Routledge, 2000, p. 26.
[162] Michael Leifer, *Singapore's Foreign Policy*, Great Britain: Routledge, 2000, p. 83.

In the immediate post Cold War context, Leifer argued that the United States had lost the will to maintain the regional balance of power, Russia had weakened militarily and was spent and Japan had become a sleeping giant, leaving the rise of China as an area of concern for ASEAN as reflected to Leifer by its policy-makers.[163] In fact, his writings sometimes indicated that it was not so much China's aggressive postures but rather the failure of countervailing big powers to manage China's rise to power: "...the region's [Southeast Asia's] states have less than full confidence in the ability of the US to sustain a countervailing role to prevent territorial change by force".[164]

The one exception to this is probably is probably the South China Sea dispute issue. Leifer's assessment of Singapore's position on this issue is that it is not so much China's aggression that caused this but it is believed that "China would not have had the temerity to seize Mischief Reef in the Spratly islands had the USA not withdrawn previously from its military bases in the Philippines".[165] Nevertheless, in May 1995, the Singapore leadership was vocal on the issue of freedom of navigation after China had seized the Mischief Reef in the Spratly Islands.[166] But even Leifer would only classify this as a "potential" conflict instead of a major one and noted dryly that Singapore is "not a claimant state".[167] In Leifer's view, there is also a concurrent failure amongst ASEAN members to establish a common position against an external claimant like China through internal dialogue, discussion and unity.[168]

---

[163] Jurgen Haacke, "Michael Leifer, the balance of power and international relations theory" in *Order and Security in Southeast Asia Essays in memory of Michael Leifer* edited by Joseph Chinyong Liow and Ralf Emmers, Great Britain, Routledge, 2006, pp. 49–50.

[164] Tommy Koh , *The Quest for World Order Perspectives of a Pragmatic Idealist*, Singapore, Federal Publications, 1998, p. 178.

[165] Michael Leifer, *Singapore's Foreign Policy*, Great Britain: Routledge, 2000, p. 160.

[166] Michael Leifer, *Singapore's Foreign Policy*, Great Britain: Routledge, 2000, p. 119.

[167] Michael Leifer, *Singapore's Foreign Policy*, Great Britain: Routledge, 2000, p. 159.

[168] Michael Leifer, The ASEAN Peace Process: A Category Mistake in *Michael Leifer: Selected Works on Southeast Asia*, edited by Chin Kin Wah and Leo Suraydinata, Singapore, ISEAS, 2005, p. 127.

In the same area, however, Tommy Koh noted a significant de-escalation of potential conflict when China acceded to the Code of Conduct on the south China Sea "in its attempt to reassure the ASEAN countries that it would not resort to the threat of the use of force to resolve the conflict territorial claims in the South China Sea, particularly in the Spratly Islands".[169]

Aside from the regional context, according to Leifer, Singapore practices self-constraint in its relationship with China, for e.g. "Singapore did not go out of its way to alienate Beijing by entering into diplomatic relations with Taiwan"; it "began with and has held continuously to a one-China policy" and Beijing has indicated its "approval".[170] All these indicated adaptability, compensation and pragmatism into Singapore's early ties with China. In the case of Taiwan, Leifer argues that without expressing sympathy for any political factions in Taiwan, Singapore's leaders have spoken out on Beijing rhetoric on the use of force but such intervention has been exceptional rather than the norm and usually done without directly criticizing China's conduct.[171] The principle of intervention is neither to interfere in China's domestic affairs nor to support Taiwan's political aspirations but to make "the obvious points that Chinese policy in Southeast Asia cannot be separated from its conduct in Northeast Asia...".[172]

In addition, Singapore's awareness of its own vulnerabilities also spilled over to its dealings with China. Leifer argued that "China has always loomed large in the calculations of Singapore's government

---

[169] Tommy Koh, "Southeast Asia" in *America's Role in Asia Asian Views*, San Francisco, Asia Foundation, 2004, p. 40.

[170] Michael Leifer, *Singapore's Foreign Policy*, Great Britain, Routledge, 2000, p. 61.

[171] Michael Leifer, Taiwan and Southeast Asia, in *Michael Leifer: Selected Works on Southeast Asia*, edited by Chin Kin Wah and Leo Suraydinata, Singapore, ISEAS, 2005, p. 279 and Michael Leifer, China in Southeast Asia: Interdependence and Accommodation, in *Michael Leifer: Selected Works on Southeast Asia*, edited by Chin Kin Wah and Leo Suraydinata, Singapore, ISEAS, 2005, p. 16.

[172] Michael Leifer, China in Southeast Asia: Interdependence and Accommodation, in *Michael Leifer: Selected Works on Southeast Asia*, edited by Chin Kin Wah and Leo Suraydinata, Singapore, ISEAS, 2005, p. 16.

because of the island's demographic profile and attendant suspicions among close neighbours" as "some three quarters of the population had comprised ethnic-Chinese of migrant origin long before independence".[173] In many ways, Singapore's reaction to the rise of China takes into account regional and domestic dynamics as well.

At the Asia Society conference in Tokyo, the Singaporean leadership also noted that "Beijing will want a peaceful international environment and constructive relations with its neighbors..." and "as China emerges as a great power, Asia–Pacific countries have the common interest to keep China peacefully engaged with other countries in the region...that will give China a deep and enduring interest in maintaining international order".[174] In Leifer's view, this was engagement in the ASEAN way.

Leifer argues that the Singapore school of balance of power is not the same as the creation of 19th century European military alliances and instead, relies on the utilization of multilateral institutions to underpin its diplomacy.[175] Its sponsorship of the ASEAN Regional Forum (ARF) engages all players in the Asia Pacific,[176] including the emerging powers of China and India. No one is left out.

Leifer's balance-of-power thus centered around emerging new players in the region like China. Despite this, he did not clearly conceptualize China as an unequivocal and exceptional threat but was reacting to his

---

[173] Michael Leifer, *Singapore's Foreign Policy*, Great Britain, Routledge, 2000, pp. 108–109.

[174] Goh Chok Tong, Keynote Address by Prime Minister, Mr Goh Chok Tong, the Asia Society Conference, on Thursday, 13 May 1993, at 9.00 am at the Hotel Okura, Tokyo Geopolitics in Asia, in the Singapore Government Press Release No. 15/May 02-1/93/05/13.

[175] Michael Leifer, *Singapore's Foreign Policy*, Great Britain, Routledge, 2000, p. 26.

[176] The ARF consists of the 10 ASEAN member states (Indonesia, Philippines, Thailand, Vietnam, Malaysia, Singapore, Brunei, Burma, Laos and Cambodia, the 12 ASEAN dialogue partners (Australia, Canada, China, Democratic People's Republic of Korea, South Korea, United States, India, Japan, New Zealand, Russia, Mongolia, and the EU) and the 1 ASEAN observer (Papua New Guinea).

instincts of the normative need to achieve equilibrium in the regional order and prescribing it for a small vulnerable state like Singapore even as China reshaped the regional environment. In analyzing China's rise in the early 1990s, Singapore's leadership detected China's increasing capability "to try to reshape any international environment that it regards as threatening its basic interests".[177]

Thus, Singapore's proactive stance in engaging all stakeholders in the region is important because balance of power in the region is "reflected in a competitive pattern of regional alignments" and the avoidance of military conflicts or confrontations is dependent on prudence by major powers that "constrains the use of military means traditionally associated with the practice of the balance of power as a policy of states".[178] Singapore's role is very much needed for ASEAN activism, especially since Leifer remains suspicious of the ability of the regional organization to go beyond aspirations and on to actual actions and decisions in coping with regional changes.

In Cold War-era Leifer writings, regional order, including an ASEAN-led one, is a "high-sounding aspiration which is difficult to define with any precision" and refers to "the existence of a stable structure of regional inter-governmental relationships informed by common assumptions about the bases of inter-state conduct".[179] In other words, Leifer's regional order refers to security obtained from states' adherence to a formal or informal set of rules. Using this definition, Leifer had great suspicions about ASEAN's ability to cope with the rise of China in the 1980s although this view was mitigated somewhat in his later writings. Cold War-era Leifer writings indicated that ASEAN

---

[177] Goh Chok Tong, Keynote Address by Prime Minister, Mr Goh Chok Tong, to the Asia Society Conference, on Thursday, 13 May 1993, at 9.00 am at the Hotel Okura, Tokyo Geopolitics in Asia, in the Singapore Government Press Release No. 15/May 02-1/93/05/13.

[178] Michael Leifer, The Balance of Power and Regional Order, in *The Balance of Power in East Asia*, edited by Michael Leifer, HK, Royal United Services Institute, 1986, p. 154.

[179] Michael Leifer, *ASEAN's Search for Regional Order Faculty Lecture 12*, Singapore, Graham Brash, 1987, p. 1.

was "not a defence community" but a "diplomatic community, if of a limited kind" and that it was beset by some kind of internal disunity arising from a number of conflicts of interests by its constituent governments.[180]

Consequently, Leifer argues that "if a regional order is difficult to define with any precision, it is even more difficult to promote because, like beauty, that ideal condition tends to reside in the eye of the beholder" and perceptions and perspectives of strategic interests and threat tend to obstruct the formation of a regional order and thus "any quest for regional order becomes an even more elusive undertaking".[181] In the English School of balance of power, each state has to be conscious of the common interest and that a regional order may not privilege equality. A stable order has to precede multilateralism and an operating norm amongst states in the region (whether institutionalized or non-institutionalized) has to exist such that each constituent adhere to some common code of conduct and expectations.

But, even Leifer admitted that differences in strategic perspectives and perceptions did not prevent the ASEAN states from pursuing the goal of a region order.[182] Ultimately, even the English balance of power has to accommodate this through being principally focused on order and based on the belief that states are constantly looking for some measures of regularity in their international activities by creating stable mechanism of habits and practices that ensure survival.[183]

---

[180] Michael Leifer, The Role and Paradox of ASEAN, in *The Balance of Power in East Asia* edited by Michael Leifer, HK, Royal United Services Institute, 1986, p. 119.

[181] Michael Leifer, *ASEAN's Search for Regional Order Faculty Lecture 12*, Singapore, Graham Brash, 1987, p. 2.

[182] Michael Leifer, *ASEAN's Search for Regional Order Faculty Lecture 12*, Singapore, Graham Brash, 1987, p. 2.

[183] Ang Cheng Guan, Michael Leifer on Cambodia and the Third Indochina Conflict, in *Order and Security in Southeast Asia Essays in memory of Michael Leifer*, edited by Joseph Chinyong Liow and Ralf Emmers, Great Britain, Routledge, 2006, p. 162.

While Leifer himself has doubts about multilateral institutions (on guard against "institutionalist optimism"[184]), in the post-Cold War context and somewhat accepted with limitations grudgingly in later Leifer writings, the balance of power within the Southeast Asian regional order has been increasingly enhanced by multilateral institutions. Singapore's active role in engagement cannot be ignored. Singapore saw great potential and utility in political engagement with China, especially if it could be located within ASEAN regional institutions and initiatives after the common stance against the Vietnamese invasion of Cambodian. Leifer labeled this as the period when Singapore "found common tactical cause with China over the regional balance of power".[185]

In constructing the regional order, Singapore has continually supported ASEAN initiatives to engage China and reshape trajectories in regional relations. For example, ASEAN and China have forged a Strategic Partnership for Peace and Prosperity with a Framework Agreement for ASEAN–China Closer Economic Relations forum for productive and open exchanges on a regular basis with the involvement of experts from academia, business and the policy community — from both sides as well as from the wider region.[186] Moving beyond Leifer's initial suspicions, ASEAN and China participated actively in various regional cooperation arrangements such as the ASEAN Plus Three, the East Asian Summit, and the Asia Pacific Economic Cooperation (APEC), as well as in the international arena — the United Nations, the World Trade Organization and other such bodies with an increased role in regional and global affairs.[187]

---

[184] Donald Emerson, Shocks of recognition: Leifer, realism, and regionalism in Southeast Asia, in *Order and Security in Southeast Asia Essays in memory of Michael Leifer*, edited by Joseph Chinyong Liow and Ralf Emmers, Great Britain, Routledge, 2006, p. 19.

[185] Michael Leifer, *Singapore's Foreign Policy*, Great Britain, Routledge, 2000, p. 115.

[186] Jusuf Wanandi, ASEAN and China Form Strategic Partnership, 15 Dec 2005, Jakarta Post. Available at http://taiwansecurity.org/News/2005/JP-151205.htm.

[187] Jusuf Wanandi, ASEAN and China Form Strategic Partnership, 15 Dec 2005, Jakarta Post. Available at http://taiwansecurity.org/News/2005/JP-151205.htm.

Leifer, writing at the turn of the century in 2000, also noted that Singapore's PM Goh himself encouraged interest in India in the mid 1990s, resulting in his initiative at the ASEAN summit in Bangkok in December 1995 to make India a dialogue partner of the Association.[188] This engagement with India is seen as an offshoot of Singapore "multi-lateralist logic"[189]; not just externally with non-ASEAN powers but also internally with ASEAN powers as this Indian initiative came with strong support from Indonesia's Suharto regime.

Kishore Mahbubani. The second individual case study in this paper is the civilizational strain of thought by Kishore Mahbubani whose landmark book *Can Asians Think?* had drawn a tremendous amount of attention in the West. Mabhubani spent 33 years in the Singapore Foreign Service from 1971 to 2004, was the Permanent Secretary at the Foreign Ministry from 1993 to 1998 and President of the UN Security Council in January 2001 and May 2002; and, for his service, he was awarded the Public Administration Medal (Gold) in 1998 and Foreign Policy Association Medal in New York in June 2004.[190]

With regards to the rise of China and India and for that matter the rise of Asia, Mahbubani's East–West tract looks at the inability of the West to develop a long-term narrative for managing relations with a rising East, incorporating elements of world history and civilization as well as practical experience gathered from his appointments in the Singapore civil service, academic and diplomatic career. In his words, "...failure to develop a viable strategy to deal with Islam or China reveals a fatal flaw in the West: an inability to come to terms with the shifts in the relative weights of civilizations..."[191]

In his view, the element of misperception has led to dissonance between the West and China because the West "obsess over the menace

---

[188] Michael Leifer, *Singapore's Foreign Policy*, Great Britain, Routledge, 2000, p. 120.

[189] Michael Leifer, *Singapore's Foreign Policy*, Great Britain, Routledge, 2000, p. 137.

[190] Kishore Mahbubani, Singapore in the United Nations Security Council, in *The Little Red Dot* edited by Tommy Koh and Chang Li Lin, Singapore, World Scientific and IPS, 2005, p. 91.

[191] Kishore Mahbubani, *Can Asians Think?*, Singapore, Times Media, 2002, p. 96.

of China"[192] whereas the Chinese consensus is convinced that the emphasis should be on becoming a developed nation by not squandering it in any military conflicts, taking into account the many times China had tried to modernize but fail. This mutual misperception highlighted by Mahbubani coincides with Prof Tommy Koh's argument of East–West misunderstanding although Koh's explanation differs by attributing East–West dissonance to the rise of East Asia catching the West unaware because it has been so "rapid and so unexpected".[193] For example, Koh obtained the impression that European participants at a colloquium in 1998 which Asia–Europe Foundation co-organized with the German newspaper *Die Zeit* on "Human Rights and Human Responsibilities" were not "sympathetic" to the point of view that "no government in human history has done so much for so many people in such a short time as the present Government of China".[194]

Aside from East–West perspectives, Mahbubani's main intra-regional observation about the rise of China is the tendency towards retaining status quo situation in the regional order: "We see the emergence of a new great power (China) but with no immediate hint of conflict. The region today is not preparing for war. It is preparing for prosperity — that is the mood and tone of the region".[195] Because of this, Mahbubani asserts that "a new consensus emerged in the region: "Let sleeping dogs lie" and "that is why we have not had any major geopolitical crisis in East Asia since March 1996, despite phenomenal historical change in our region".[196]

---

[192] Kishore Mahbubani, *The New Asian Hemisphere*, New York, Public Affairs, 2008, p. 81.

[193] Tommy Koh, *The United States and East Asia*, Singapore, Times Academic Press, 1995, p. 2.

[194] Tommy Koh, Asian Values Reconsidered, in *Asia and Europe Essays and Speeches by Tommy Koh*, edited by Yeo Lay Hwee and Asad Latif, Singapore, Asia Europe Foundation, 2000, p. 57.

[195] Kishore Mahbubani, *Can Asians Think?*, Singapore, Times Media, 2002, p. 159.

[196] Kishore Mabhubani, *Can Asians Think?*, Singapore, Times Media, 2002, p. 160.

One example that Mahbubani gives to demonstrate this is China's maintenance of status quo in its nuclear arsenal through its unwillingness move more than half of its 400 nuclear warheads out of secure location, not keeping operational warheads at hair-trigger alert and its less enthusiastic attitude in modernizing the nuclear arsenal, resulting in the non-development of nuclear stockpile for more than 20 years.[197] In this sense, Mahbubani is less worried about China's geostrategic threat than the outcome of the changing pecking order in East Asia. Essentially, the one limitation that Mahbubani detects in the future of East Asia is not the rise of China or India itself but the shape and form of the new pecking order it would bring about. Foremost on his thoughts is Sino–Japanese relations:

"But Asians also accept hierarchy. When this is not violated, peace can reign. The fascination of Sino–Japanese relations is in deciding who should view whom as number one. Economically, Japan is far ahead, but in political and military terms China carries more weight. Japan is more stable than China in the short term, and China needs Japanese economic aid and investment. But Japan needs China's market, as well as social stability in China. While Japan's culture is derived from China, Japan carries more weight in the international hierarchy. So who determines who is number one?".[198]

Like Mahbubani, Koh is worried about regional big power competition and hope for reconciliation between East Asia's two largest power. In his view, historical memories is the main culprit that makes the competition picture in Northeast Asia "less satisfactory" because "historic reconciliation of the kind that occurred between England, France and Germany has not taken place between China and Japan or between Japan and Korea" and "the ghosts of the past continue to haunt the

---

[197] Kishore Mahbubani, *The New Asian Hemisphere*, New York, Public Affairs, 2008, pp. 81–82.
[198] Kishore Mahbubani, *Can Asians Think?*, Singapore, Times Media, 2002, pp. 154–155.

triangular relationship between China, Japan and Korea".[199] Koh suggests a long-term solution for this situation — to have "visionary leaders" who can "simultaneously bury the past and inspire the peoples of East Asia with the vision of a New Asia".[200]

All three are in agreement when it comes to big power politics. Mahbubani's view above on the interactions and interdependence of great power with its own dynamics coincides with Prof Tommy Koh's view on one of the pillars of Singapore's foreign policy which "does not seek to change the world as it is and not as we would like it to be".[201] In other words, Koh argues that big power politics will have its own dynamics. Agreeing with this view, Leifer extends this argument to the whole of ASEAN, in that ASEAN was established as an enterprise "in the full knowledge that certain underlying facts of political life could not be changed at will, including the sense of vulnerability of some member states".[202] Leifer added: "Singapore is hardly in a position to manage the relationship between China and South-East Asia. It is obliged to use whatever influence it can muster in the cause of a policy of engagement deemed to serve the island-state's interests better than any other policy option."[203] This is part of his fundamental belief that developments at the global and regional level impact those at the sub-regional level or what he called "balance of extra-regional influences".[204]

---

[199] Tommy Koh, What Can East Asia Learn from the European Union, in *Asia and Europe Essays and Speeches by Tommy Koh*, edited by Yeo Lay Hwee and Asad Latif, Singapore, Asia Europe Foundation, 2000, p. 60.

[200] Tommy Koh, What Can East Asia Learn from the European Union, in *Asia and Europe Essays and Speeches by Tommy Koh*, edited by Yeo Lay Hwee and Asad Latif, Singapore, Asia Europe Foundation, 2000, p. 60.

[201] Tommy Koh, *The Quest for World Order Perspectives of a Pragmatic Idealist*, Singapore, Federal Publications, 1998, p. 177.

[202] Michael Leifer, *ASEAN's Search for Regional Order Faculty Lecture 12*, Singapore, Graham Brash, 1987, p.18.

[203] Michael Leifer, *Singapore's Foreign Policy*, Great Britain, Routledge, 2000, p. 121.

[204] Jurgen Haacke, Michael Leifer, the balance of power and international relations theory, in *Order and Security in Southeast Asia Essays in memory of Michael Leifer*, edited by Joseph Chinyong Liow and Ralf Emmers, Great Britain, Routledge, 2006, p. 47.

Tommy Koh. If big power politics cannot be changed either by Singapore or ASEAN, then a pragmatic strategy is needed cope with its impact and changes. Pragmatism is a running theme in Prof Tommy Koh's thoughts. Koh is Ambassador-At-Large, Ministry of Foreign Affairs, Chairman of the Institute of Policy Studies and served as Singapore's Permanent Representative to the UN (New York) from 1968 to 1971 and from 1974 to 1984 before becoming ambassador to the US from 1984 to 1990; Professor Koh was also the President of the Third UN Conference on the Law of the Sea from 1981 to 1982 and Dean of Faculty of Law of the National University of Singapore from 1971 to 1974.[205]

Like Mahbubani, Koh also comes from a mixed academic–practitioner background but he is a self-declared pragmatic idealist who practices qualified idealism with the important core values of the optimistic view of human nature and its belief in the possibility of cooperation qualified by the role of international and regional regimes in curbing the use of force and restraining excessive competition; in the process rejecting the notions that national interest is the only basis for state decision-making and that the ends justify the means of using deception to achieve one's goals. In Koh's view, there should be a moral component to diplomacy and international legality has to be balanced with morality while national interests alone cannot determine good diplomacy.

In the mid-1990s, Koh made the argument that Asia Pacific Economic Cooperation (APEC)'s inclusion of China was beneficial to "assist China in integrating itself into the world economy" to lock China into the region so that large economies like Japan and "the United States and East Asia can together build an Asia-Pacific region which is prosperous and stable".[206] Agreeing with this view, Leifer argues that there is also a conscious preference amongst Singapore's policy-makers for a politically stable China to avoid the "prospect of a flow

---

[205] Tommy Koh, Eight Lessons on Negotiations, in *The Little Red Dot,* edited by Tommy Koh and Chang Li Lin, Singapore, World Scientific and IPS, 2005, p. 199.
[206] Tommy Koh, *The United States and East Asia,* Singapore, Times Academic Press, 1995, pp. 20–21.

of refugees and regional turmoil".[207] In other words, nobody in the region wants a failed state or economy in China and there is a conscious effort to co-prosper with China herself. In scenario-planning, Koh noted that smaller neighbours of China hope that China will continue to "pursue a policy of good neighbourliness and not become a region bully".[208] There was a sense that big countries should display some sense of morality in self-restraint while unmitigated self-interests should be tampered with regional peace and order.

As a member of the ASEAN–China Eminent Persons Group (EPG) from Singapore, Koh was contributive to a report that assessed relations between China and ASEAN from 1990 to 2005 and proposed a new vision and roadmap from 2005 to 2020. This report reflected the optimism, role of cooperation and coded messages of regional peace envisioned by Koh as a pragmatic idealist. The report made it clear that while ASEAN and China will deepen and strengthen their strategic relationship, they will adopt "an open and inclusive approach" in promoting regional peace and security regional peace and security with other dialogue partners, including the US, Japan, India and the European Union (EU).[209] Conversely, these powers must also not regard East Asia as a threat but an opportunity and thus its "growing stake in East Asia's prosperity" so that the "American political and security commitment to the region will endure".[210]

Having an open and inclusive approach, proved to be useful in restraining excessive competition and self-seeking conduct within the region which is beneficial for a small state like Singapore. It also reflected the principles of morality in terms of justice (restraining aggression), equality (all-encompassing regional order including small

---

[207] Michael Leifer, *Singapore's Foreign Policy,* Great Britain, Routledge, 2000, p. 120.

[208] Tommy Koh, *The United States and East Asia,* Singapore, Times Academic Press, 1995, p. 63.

[209] Tommy Koh, Rodolfo Severino and Jusuf Wanadi, China and ASEAN: Roadmap to Future. 14 December 2005. The *Business Times* [Accessed 1 June 2008]. Available at www.ips.org.sg.

[210] Tommy Koh, *The United States and East Asia,* Singapore, Times Academic Press, 1995, p. 16.

states) and cooperation (deepening strategic relationship and confidence-building measures). All these qualities gravitate towards moderation and the assumption that states are not absolutist — neither so moral that it needs no regional order nor so aggressive that they are constantly at war. An open and inclusive regional order will promote mutual accommodation and benefits.

Koh also applied his open and inclusive approach to the rise of India. In his view, with the rise of India and the growing connectivity between India, Australia and New Zealand, and Northeast and Southeast Asia, it was logical for ASEAN to launch the East Asia Summit (EAS) which brings together ASEAN+3+3 (Australia, New Zealand, and India) and, apart from its economic logic, the EAS forum has great strategic significance because Asia's peace will depend on the ability of China, Japan, and India to live at peace with one another.[211] In turn, Koh also recommends that these major Asian powers are balanced with US might and that the US should remain engaged with the region as a unit:

"ASEAN is now being courted by all the major powers in the region — China, Japan, South Korea, and India. Given that other countries are seeking influence in ASEAN, it would be in the US interest, as well as in the interest of ASEAN, for the US to engage with ASEAN as a collective unit in order to continue to constructively influence the region".[212]

An open and inclusive approach to regionalism is derived from a pragmatic foreign policy based on the "one lodestar — the security and prosperity of Singapore"[213] is applied here. This is because Singapore's geo-strategic thinking does not think that they it can rely solely on a regional framework of normative behaviour to survive and needs to go

---

[211] Tommy Koh, ASEAN at 40: Perception and Reality, in the US Korea Council website [Accessed on 2 June 2008]. Available at www.uskoreacouncil.org/.../ASEANat40PerceptionandReality.doc.

[212] Tommy Koh, "Southeast Asia" in *America's Role in Asia Asian Views*, San Francisco, Asia Foundation, 2004, p. 38.

[213] Tommy Koh , *The Quest for World Order Perspectives of a Pragmatic Idealist*, Singapore, Federal Publications, 1998, p. 177.

beyond the immediate region to engage non-East Asian powers for extra security and guarantees. In other words, consensus-building based on the inclusion of all stakeholders (not necessarily only East Asian powers only) forms the foundation of Koh's approach to multilateralism.

Evaluation. In evaluating the thoughts of the three thinkers, it may be possible to analytically frame it within the rubric of well-known criticisms of Singapore's foreign policy by other regional states; three such examples will be examined here. Some of these criticisms are offshoots or byproducts of the principles enunciated by the three thinkers covered in this article. The first example is a charge against Singapore's foreign policy by countries in the region that Singapore is "over-legalistic" and "fixated with facts".[214] the above materials on the cold-hard *Leiferesque* realist approach to Koh's institution-building emphasis, one can detect the rational model at work here in conceptualizing Singapore's relations with other states.

By maximizing benefits while lowering costs, Singapore's diplomacy may give others the impression that it is overly rule-bound and institutionally conforming. It is important to stress that this is a perception and impression on receptors of Singapore's Foreign Policy and may not be a reflection of intentions. Sometimes, at the field level, given the organizational process and standard operating procedures, it may be unavoidable that if enunciated principles are applied faithfully, it may give others the impression of being "over-legalistic" and "fixated with facts".

While such misperceptions may be forwarded by some countries, on the whole however, Singapore enjoys a well-regarded reputation for being fair and equitable. The reason is precisely due to Singapore's diplomats (including Koh and Mahbubani) have been generally known in the diplomatic circle for their strategic vision, their ability to understand and analyze the trends and dynamics in the region and their ability to propose constructive initiatives and thus rewarded with the

---

[214] Ministry of Foreign Affairs (MFA), Transcript of Remarks On Malaysia–Singapore Relations by Minister for Foreign Affairs, Prof S Jayakumar in Parliament. 16 May 2002, [Accessed on 15 September 2008]. Available at http://app-stg1.mfa.gov.sg/2006/lowres/press/view_press.asp?post_id=1262.

Chairmanship of the UN Convention for the Law of the Sea, a role in the UN Security Council and other contributions.

In particular, Koh has instituted a strong belief in the superiority of an accurate technical understanding of international law in achieving success in multilateral diplomacy and easing tensions.[215] In this way, legalism and facts are thus transformed into strong points for Singapore's foreign policy. Its adherence to rules and norms also denote the consistency of the application of Singapore's foreign policy.

The second critique of Singapore's foreign policy centers on excessive pragmatism. Pragmatism in its China policy is symbolized by the way Singapore dealt with China and Taiwan. In 1967, in order to overcome Singapore's lack of training space and not to be completely dependent on the Israelis for assistance in the training of its military, Singapore started discussions with the Taiwanese for use of their training areas but, when Taiwan set up its trade office in Singapore two years later, Singapore insisted that this exchange of trade missions did not entail formal diplomatic recognition of each other.

Critics may seize on this example as being calculative through the maximization of self-interest and benefit while minimizing costs according to the bound rationality model. However, very often, Singapore is working with the restraints of being a small player which all three (Leifer, Koh and Mahbubani) acknowledges. Pragmatism is as much geopolitically determined by its natural attributes as it is a conscious byproduct of Singapore's survival instinct. This is strongly put across by Leifer's doubts about multilateralism, Koh's cautious caveat of strategic and cautious pragmatism and Mahbubani's tract on the inability to change the directions of Chinese accumulation of power and economic development. But is the criticism valid?

Seen empirically, Singapore has adhered strictly to its one-China policy and never established formal diplomatic ties with Taiwan, even though relations have continued to be friendly and mutually beneficial.

---

[215] Alan Chong, Singapore's foreign policy beliefs as 'Abridged Realism': pragmatic and liberal prefixes in the foreign policy thought of Rajaratnam, Lee, Koh, and Mahbubani in International Relations of the Asia-Pacific, Vol. 6 No. 2 (Japan: Oxford Journal), 2006, p. 291.

In this sense, Singapore's pragmatism has paid off, giving it one of the few countries in the world with the unique position of having good relations with both China and Taiwan, even hosting their unification talks.

In many ways, Mahbubani alludes to the dividends of Singapore's pragmatism, paid off because Singapore understands the pecking order in the region and its position in it. It does not pretend to challenge China's interest. But one cannot charge it with being overly pragmatic because, from time to time, Singapore is prepared to stand up to China (or for that matter other great powers) if it needs to (e.g. vocalizing its views on the South China Sea dispute) but doing it cautiously, exceptionally and often strategically with gentle persuasion.

A third criticism of Singapore's foreign policy is related to the first two — lack of cultural understanding, arising from the legalistic approach and a pragmatic instinct for survival. While legality and facts are important to Singapore, Mahbubani's thoughts also indicate its sensitivity to culture, identity and civilizational features. Unlike Koh and Leifer who are stronger functionalists, Mahbubani also looks at historical precedents and regional identity in formulating his thoughts. Thus, rationality in Singapore's neofunctionalist institutionalism does have its limits with a softer edge in culture, history and civilization.

Mahbubani's constructivist preoccupation with pecking order may allude to the fact that Singapore's foreign policy may be skilful in recognizing Asian norms, cultural nuance and identity. Pragmatism works if it is the normative behaviour in the region, perhaps symbolized by the so-called intra-regional normative ASEAN Way. If Singapore does not recognize these cultural norms, would it have deferred diplomatic recognition of China only after Indonesia had done so based on its own internal ethnic structure and sensitivity to regional states? One can argue that Singapore is precisely privy to the regional cultural norms *because* it has a multiracial makeup that reflects the major civilizations, cultures and religions in the region, a point that Mahbubani makes clear.

Conclusion. The eclectic nature of these three schools of thought represents the multiplicity of identities in the cosmopolitan society of Singapore and different strategic conceptions. The fluidity of regional dynamics has also modified previous perceptions. For example, Leifer considered India to be "diplomatically distant" in secondary importance.[216] Such perspectives have depended on inheritors of the Leifer School of thought to update and bring it up to speed to the contemporary context. Because even Leifer had to acknowledge Singapore's attention in promoting India as a dialogue partner of ASEAN and supporting India's membership in the ASEAN Regional Forum (ARF) and these happened even before India had greatly expended its energies and expanded international reach to encompass Southeast Asia, especially in the post-911 increased security cooperation with the US, Japan and other global players under the rubric of the War on Terror.

In fact, India has moved into regional prominence. As a first step, India has acceded to the Treaty of Amity and Cooperation (TAC).[217] Singapore has been quick to balance China engagement with India outreach through the initiative at the ASEAN summit in Bangkok in December 1995 to make India a dialogue partner of the Association, drawing immediate support from ASEAN countries like Indonesia. India and ASEAN are also forging a similar prominent role in global and regional politics. Singapore's self-reliance in taking the initiative in balancing all regional powers is the second pillar of its foreign policy that places premium on self-help.[218]

At the 4th India-ASEAN Summit in Kuala Lumpur, both sides discussed the global issue of terrorism and pledged to intensify cooperation to fight the menace. This was exemplified by Malaysian Prime Minister Badawi's message: "Terrorism is still a major threat to our collective security in this region. We are saddened with the loss of lives as a result of the recent bombings in India."[219] He also said it is timely to proceed with implementing some form of concrete cooperation based on the

---

[216] Chin Kin Wah, The foreign policy of Singapore, in *Order and Security in Southeast Asia Essays in memory of Michael Leifer*, edited by Joseph Chinyong Liow and Ralf Emmers, Great Britain, Routledge, 2006, p. 211.

[217] Tommy Koh, Southeast Asia, in *America's Role in Asia Asian Views*, San Francisco, Asia Foundation, 2004, p. 40.

[218] Tommy Koh , *The Quest for World Order Perspectives of a Pragmatic Idealist*, Singapore, Federal Publications, 1998, p. 177.

[219] Nandita Mallik, India A Powerhouse: ASEAN, 13 December 2005 [Accessed on 11 March 2006]. Available at http://www.rediff.com/money/2005/dec/13ASEAN2.htm.

ASEAN–India Declaration on Cooperation to Combat International Terrorism which was adopted in Bali.[220]

In terms of worldview, both ASEAN and China have agreed to practice the "policy of open regionalism" characterized by the ASEAN–China strategic partnership and an emphasis on intensified engagement of civil society in regional community building, catalyzed by greater people-to-people interaction and cooperation with their voices brought to the attention of governments.[221] In this aspect, a second track ASEAN–China collaboration is encouraged and facilitated by governments and invited to develop ideas and make concrete suggestions to substantiate the strategic partnership.[222] ASEAN and India also aligned their security worldviews during the Vientiane Summit in 2004 and signed the ASEAN–India partnership for peace, progress and shared prosperity which endorsed a Plan of Action to implement it.[223]

There are also differences in intensity of faith and views of multilateral institutions in building regional order. If realism represented one extreme end of a scale and multilateralism represented the other end, Leifer and his lingering doubts about multilateral institutions would probably be placed nearer to the realist end while Koh and his affinity for idealism based on consensus-building would also be more supportive of multilateralism with some caution in the area of national interests. Mahbubani would be seeking aspects of both ends for the construction of a new pecking order. The pecking order is reflective of his fundamental belief that there is no inevitability of a clash between great powers as long as world leaders refine their vision of relative power changes by shifting away from the idea that the

---

[220] Nandita Mallik, India A Powerhouse: ASEAN, 13 December 2005 [Accessed on 11 March 2006]. Available at http://www.rediff.com/money/2005/dec/13ASEAN2.htm.

[221] Jusuf Wanandi, ASEAN and China Form Strategic Partnership, 15 Dec 2005, Jakarta Post. Available at http://taiwansecurity.org/News/2005/JP-151205.htm.

[222] Jusuf Wanandi, ASEAN and China Form Strategic Partnership, 15 Dec 2005, Jakarta Post. Available at http://taiwansecurity.org/News/2005/JP-151205.htm.

[223] Nandita Mallik, India A Powerhouse: ASEAN, 13 December 2005, [Accessed on 11 March 2006]. Available at http://www.rediff.com/money/2005/dec/13ASEAN2.htm.

Western realist intellectual and cultural hegemony are unchallenge-able qualities.[224]

Despite their differences, the four schools of thought stressed similar messages with some convergence — that Singapore's long-term survival is dependence on being a proactive and sociable member of a regional order, be it with a core that is accomodationist, balance of power, civiliza-tionally-oriented or idealistically pragmatic. Singapore's policy-makers have equated security risks with the consequences of a collapse of the normative framework governing the regional order. This normative framework, according to Leifer, requires a "set of shared assumptions about the interrelationships among resident and external states".[225]

While Leifer has some reservations about the effectiveness of mul-tilateral institutions (for e.g. ARF as an "imperfect diplomatic instru-ment"[226]), all are in favor of balancing the interests of a small state with the community at large. The effectiveness of multilateral ASEAN institutions like ASEAN+3 amongst other ASEAN fora, Mabhubani argued, is that Northeast Asian leaders can also "meet comfortably and discuss common challenges"[227] and remain peaceful in a region which Singapore is embedded in.

Leifer noted that the engagement of major powers in Northeast Asia is an such enduring feature that it was already in place during the Cold War when ASEAN institutions were far weaker and, in this, credit should also be given major powers in the region for containing conflicts

---

[224] Alan Chong, Singapore's foreign policy beliefs as 'Abridged Realism': prag-matic and liberal prefixes in the foreign policy thought of Rajaratnam, Lee, Koh, and Mahbubani, in International Relations of the Asia-Pacific, Vol. 6 No. 2, Japan, Oxford Journal, 2006, p. 298.

[225] Michael Leifer, The Balance of Power and Regional Order, in *The Balance of Power in East Asia,* edited by Michael Leifer, HK, Royal United Services Institute, 1986, p. 152.

[226] Michael Leifer, *Selected Works on Southeast Asia,* edited by Chin Kin Wah and Leo Suryadinata, Singapore, Institute of Southeast Asian Studies, 2005, p. 156.

[227] Kishore Mahbubani, *The New Asian Hemisphere,* New York, Public Affairs, 2008, p. 84.

"within manageable bounds and within a framework of constraint imposed by the sense of prudence".[228] Leifer also admitted that, despite his doubt about multilateral institutions in fostering regional order, ASEAN has the "attendant cohesion displayed in crises" and that its "institutionalized dialogues with industrialized states are a reflection of its international standing".[229]

Mahbubani and Koh also agree on looking at history to determine patterns of Chinese regional behaviour. Mahbubani noted that "for such a large country as China, it is surprising that China has a minimal imperial tradition outside its borders" and that, in many periods of its history, "China could have easily expanded its empire beyond its borders but it expressed no desire to do so".[230]

Without being deterministic about zero-sum realism in great power diplomacy, Koh argues that, if history was a guide (albeit an uncertain one), China would behave in a relatively benign manner as it had done in the past when it was powerful.[231] Like Mahbubani, Koh argues that "looking to the past for lessons to extrapolate to the future is a good start"[232] but being a pragmatist, he also warned that this should not be excessive. Even during the Cold War, Leifer, who was arguably more realist than the other two individuals in this paper, opined that East Asia was not a region where any one state was able to "exercise a dominating influence" and where the balance of between global and local adversaries is not "decisively weighted".[233]

---

[228] Michael Leifer, The Balance of Power and Regional Order, in *The Balance of Power in East Asia,* edited by Michael Leifer, HK, Royal United Services Institute, 1986, p. 154.

[229] Michael Leifer, *ASEAN's Search for Regional Order Faculty Lecture 12,* Singapore, Graham Brash, 1987, p. 15.

[230] Kishore Mahbubani, *Beyond the Age of Innocence,* New York, Public Affairs, 2005, p. 100.

[231] Tommy Koh, *The United States and East Asia,* Singapore, Times Academic Press, 1995, p. 75.

[232] Tommy Koh, *The United States and East Asia,* Singapore, Times Academic Press, 1995, pp. 74–75.

[233] Michael Leifer, The Balance of Power and Regional Order, in *The Balance of Power in East Asia,* edited by Michael Leifer, HK, Royal United Services Institute, 1986, p. 143.

By bringing China into the family of nations through the construction of multilateral institutions, Koh argues that China "will have to learn to play by the international rules and to act responsibly...with the best possible outcome for the United States, Japan and China to co-operate to find a balance of power in the Asia-Pacific".[234] Koh believes that engagement brings about exposure to regional and international opinions which is important because he believes that "no country is immune from the pressure of world opinion".[235]

Engaging China and embracing her as a member of the family of nation is very much similar to Leifer's argument for engagement within a regional order and Mahbubani's search for a new consensus.[236] Arising from Koh's seventh pillar of Singapore's foreign policy which is the willingness of Singapore to work with other countries to ensure a stable and peaceful environment in the region, Koh argues unequivocally that he believed "it is better to engage China than to contain her" and that "it is not possible for either the United States or the United States and Japan, acting together, to stop China's progress".[237]

Koh and the ASEAN-China EPG had also entrenched the principle of operating within a regional order as one of great importance. While ASEAN wished to have the best possible relations with China, the grouping acknowledged that there are other stakeholders (India, Japan, US and EU) in Southeast Asia and would cooperate with all the stakeholders to promote regional peace and security.[238] A successful relationship with Southeast Asia (Singapore included) will be the evidence that China's rise will be peaceful and non-threatening to the region.

---

[234] Tommy Koh, *The United States and East Asia,* Singapore, Times Academic Press, 1995, p. 75.
[235] Jurgen Haacke, *ASEAN's Diplomatic and Security Culture,* London and NY, Routledge, 2005, p. 90.
[236] Tommy Koh , *The Quest for World Order Perspectives of a Pragmatic Idealist,* Singapore, Federal Publications, 1998, p. 178.
[237] Tommy Koh, *The United States and East Asia,* Singapore, Times Academic Press, 1995, p. 75.
[238] Tommy Koh, Rodolfo Severino and Jusuf Wanadi, China and ASEAN: Roadmap to Future, 14 December 2005, *The Business Times* [Accessed on 1 June 2008]. Available at www.ips.org.sg.

Mahbubani's thoughts complement this because he fundamentally believes that China's rise will be peaceful and that the threat is a form of misperception by the West: "Given the increasing sophistication of Chinese political discourse, it is remarkable how few Western minds understand the scope and significance of the changes China has made. Not many Chinese are willing to speak openly about their frustration with Western pundits, who continue to try to paint China in black and white terms".[239] Unlike the West, the East including Singapore and ASEAN in this sense have less problems understanding the subtleties of China and India's rise engaging them in fora where leaders can talk about regional issues freely.

Mahbubani also pointed out that post-Deng China continued to support the new emerging consensus amongst East Asian nations for regional order: "Deng Xiaoping's pragmatic wisdom has outlived him, becoming firmly embedded in Chinese political culture" which "explains why China's relations with virtually all of its neighbors have actually improved since he died".[240]

The involvement of India in ASEAN fora is even more obvious given Mahbubani's view of India as a natural meeting point for all major civilizations. In his view, India has a natural role to "be a bridge between the East and the West" with its Bollywood's ability "to overcome the Hindu–Muslim divide" and its historical accommodation of "so many civilizations-including Hindu, Buddhist, Islamic, and Christian cultures — and how most of them have lived in peace with each other for most of its history".[241] Koh agrees and argued that given "India's long and benign historical ties with Southeast Asia, India could play a constructive role in the [region's] security equation".[242]

---

[239] Kishore Mahbubani, *The New Asian Hemisphere,* New York, Public Affairs, 2008, pp. 145–146.

[240] Kishore Mahbubani, *The New Asian Hemisphere,* New York, Public Affairs, 2008, p. 219.

[241] Kishore Mahbubani, *The New Asian Hemisphere,* New York, Public Affairs, 2008, pp. 170, 171

[242] Tommy Koh, *The United States and East Asia,* Singapore, Times Academic Press, 1995, p. 76.

Finally, even the most pragmatic of the three, Prof Tommy Koh, does not unquestioningly convert to an idealist without the necessary caution in the form of pragmatism. In fact some commentators had described him as an idealist operating within a realist regional order and framework.[243] He also subscribed to the mantra that "one should always have ideals, but be prepared to adjust to reality".[244] At times, all three revert back to Leifer's English school which incorporates realist elements of national interests in searching for the regional order and the assumption that a multilateral organization like ARF is dependent on a preexisting stable order and that it is not in a position to create it.[245] All of them recognize the limits of multilateralism but understand its necessity.

---

[243] Tommy Koh, *The Quest for World Order Perspectives of a Pragmatic Idealist,* Singapore, Federal Publications, 1998, p. xiv.

[244] Tommy Koh, *The Quest for World Order Perspectives of a Pragmatic Idealist,* Singapore, Federal Publications, 1998, p. xxi.

[245] Amitav Archaya, Do norms and identity matter? Community and power in Southeast Asia's regional order, in *Order and Security in Southeast Asia Essays in Memory of Michael Leifer,* edited by Joseph Chinyong Liow and Ralf Emmers, Great Britain, Routledge, 2006, p. 86.

Chapter 8

The Rise of China and India and Its Implications for Southeast Asia: A Thai Perspective

Prapat Thepchatree

This chapter analyzes the rise of China and India and its implications for Southeast Asia from a Thai perspective. It is organized in three parts. The first part focuses on the rise of China and is sub-divided as follows: China's ascendancy and its implications for Asia; Beijing's grand strategy; the triangular relationship between China, US, and Southeast Asia; China–ASEAN relations; and ASEAN's strategy towards the rise of its Northeast Asian giant neighbor. The second part of the chapter focuses on the rise of India and is sub-divided as follows: a comparison between the ascendancy of China and India; the concept of "Chindia" (the potential synergy and synthesis of the two Asian giants and conceivably a condominium in Asia); possible economic, geopolitical and military competition between these two rising powers; and more specifically Sino–Indian competition in Southeast Asia. The third and last part of the chapter briefly analyzes various Thai outlooks towards the two Asian giants.

I would argue that Thailand has a strategic culture which is acutely and skillfully attuned to shifting balances of power and is indeed the only Asian country (besides Japan) which was not colonized by the West. If Thailand were to adhere to this pragmatic tradition of adapting and taking advantage of emerging configurations of power, the nation should not encounter serious problems with the rise of China and India. Just as it has negotiated around British and French competition in colonial Southeast Asia, allied with Japan during World War II, and befriended the US superpower again as an alliance partner, and aligned with China against Vietnam's occupation of Cambodia in 1978, Thailand will in the same pragmatic manner make a virtue out of necessity by coping and benefiting from the rise of China and India.

Rise of China and its Implications to Asia[246]

Many studies have highlighted the exponential and remarkable expansion of the Chinese economy. One analyst even asserted that by 2025 the size of Chinese economy will equal that of the US economy.[247] Another study noted that China's GDP in 2000 was around US$5 trillion while the US GDP was twice that size in the same year. Indeed, if, all things equal, the Chinese economy were to grow continuously at the rate of 7.5 percent and if the American rate of growth remains at 2.5 percent, China would catch up and match the size of the US economy by 2015.[248]

Foreign direct investment (FDI) flows to the Chinese mainland is equally impressive. China surpassed the US as the world's number one

---

[246] For an overview of the rise of China, see Robert S. Ross, China and the Stability of East Asia, in Robert S. Ross (ed.), *East Asia in Transition*, Armonk, N.Y., M.E. Sharpe, 1995; Soon-Bum Ahnm, China as Number One, *Current History* (September 2001); Gaye Christoffersen, China and the Asia-Pacific, *Asian Survey*, Vol. 36(11) (November 1996); Andrew Nathan and Robert Ross, *The Great Wall and the Empty Fortress,* N.Y., W.W. Norton; E. Economy, China's Rise in Southeast Asia: Implications for Japan and the United States *Council on Foreign Relations*. Available at <www.cfr.org>.

[247] J. Kugler, *et al.*, Power Transitions and Alliances in the 21st Century, *Asian Perspective*, 25(3), 2001, 5–29.

[248] W. Bert, *The United States, China and Southeast Asian Security,* Palgrave Macmillan, 2003.

destination with FDI amounting to US$53 billion U.S. dollars; in contrast, the American economy received only US$40 billion.[249] Moreover, China is also surpassing the US as number one in consumption:

- In 2003, China consumed 382 million tons of grain; whereas the U.S. consumed only 278 million tons;
- In the same year, China consumed 258 million tons steel — a very important indicator for industrial development In contrast, the US consumed only 140 million tons of steel;
- The pattern is the same for coal in the same year: the US consumed 574 million tons; China consumed about 800 million tons of the same item;
- China has 269 million mobile phone users whereas the US only 159 million.
- China also has more than 374 million TV sets while the US only 243 million.[250]

The pattern and picture are clear across the board: China today is surpassing the US as the number one country of consumerism. Arguably, this is a very important indicator for the East Asian giant to evolve into an economic superpower and leader. China is also narrowing the gap very rapidly especially in R&D. Several surveys indicate that American technological domination has suffered from relative decline. American scientific research publications decrease from 61 percent in 1983 to only 29 percent in 2003. At the same time, Chinese research publications have dramatically increased.[251] In the arena of military capability, Beijing has increased its military budget markedly and is ranked number three in the world. And there is a prediction that Chinese naval force in the Asia-Pacific will surpass the US within 10 years.

---

[249] China's appeal overshadows US, *The Nation*, June 29, 2004, 6B.
[250] China replacing US as world's leading consumer *Bangkok Post*, March 6, 2005, 5; China overtakes US as biggest consumer, *Bangkok Post*, February 18, 2005, B7.
[251] US losing its scientific edge, *Bangkok Post*, May 4, 2004,7.

Military power

Several analyses claim that there has been a fundamental transformation in the power structure of the global system. More particularly, the Asian power structure is being transformed by the rise of China. But the big question is: how will the ascendancy of Chinese power manifest itself? Theoretically, the components and sinews of power which underpin a superpower are: military, economic and cultural.[252]

According to Beijing, its military budget for 2007 was around US$45 billion, an increase of 18 percent which is probably one of the highest rates of increase in history. However, some analysts claim that the Chinese official figures are not quite correct because if they are calculated by using Purchasing Power Parity (PPP), the real figure of its military budget would be considerably higher at US$450 billion — much closer to the US military budget of around US$500–600 billion.[253] Therefore, this new estimate has alarmed Washington about the rise of Chinese military power which will challenge US hegemony. In recent years, it has becoming increasingly clear that the Washington is trying to pursue military containment strategy against Beijing.

Economic power

Chinese economic power is also increasing rapidly. The rate of its economic growth averaged 10 percent since 1990 — among the highest in the world. If China is merely a small country, such an increase would have had no global impact. But China has a "jumbo" sized economy. The country has a gargantuan population of 1.3 billion and the magnitude of its growth is surpassing almost all countries in the world except the US. The Chinese GDP today, if calculated by the PPP principle, is around US$5 trillion — already half of the US GDP. However, the Chinese rate of growth is much higher than the US superpower. If the Chinese economy were to continue expanding at such an impressive rate, it will

---

[252] Z. Brzezinski, *Grand Chessboard*, New York, Basic Books, 1997, Chapter 1.
[253] J. Tkacik, A Chinese Military Superpower? webmemo#1389, March 8, 2007, Heritage Foundation.

probably equal and then surpass the size of American economy around 2025. China then will become the largest economy in the world.[254] And it is reasonable to expect that any country with the largest economic power in the world will seek to translate it into political influence.

From a historical perspective, China's economic resurgence can be considered normal or even *déjà vu* since because its economy was the world's largest for a millennium before the advent of the Western Renaissance, Age of Enlightenment, imperialism and colonialism. In 1600, Chinese economy was the largest on earth accounting for 30 percent of the global economy.[255] After a few centuries of relative decline, a resurgent China is reclaiming its previous place and status in the global economy. China now is surpassing Japan as number three in the world in terms of trade (the US is number one and Germany number two). If we were to use PPP principle, China might well have surpassed Germany as number two.

China is expanding its FDI in other countries with a focus on natural resource development and energy, which are high on the nation's demands. Its strategy on FDI is to link it with foreign economic assistance and soft loans. Spearheaded by this strategy, Chinese influence rapidly increases, particularly in Southeast Asia, Africa, and Central Asia. In 2005, the amount of Chinese investment abroad is more than US$10 billion. As for FDI, the Chinese Mainland is now the world's number one destination.[256] On economic assistance, China has changed its role from recipient to donor country. In 2006, China organized the China–Africa Summit with more than 48 African leaders. And China impressed with a huge aid package to Africa valued at more than US$5.5 billion.[257]

Cultural power

The third power component that will propel China to become a balanced and full-fledged super power is cultural or "soft" power. China

---

[254] Kugler, op.cit.
[255] Special report on China and its region, *Economist,* March 31, 2007.
[256] Ibid.
[257] Ibid.

would like to expand its cultural influence by competing against Western values — and more specifically America culture — which underpin their political structures and ideas, economic systems, and human rights agenda. In the long term, it is anticipated that China will challenge the US as the leader in the arena and marketplace for global ideas and cultures.

In the past, economic development policy of the developing countries usually followed the US-inspired "Washington Consensus" which emphasizes market mechanism, deregulation, free trade, and democracy. But some developing countries have already switched to the so-called "Beijing Consensus" which emphasizes the Chinese developmental model undergirded by the central role of the state to promote and manage rapid economic growth minus liberal democracy. However, China still has a long way to go to compete with the US in terms of cultural appeal globally. Certain aspects of American mass culture in fashion, sports and entertainment are still emulated globally whereas Chinese culture cannot challenge American culture at the global level yet.

According to John Mearsheimer,[258] the economic rise of China will eventually lead to Sino–US serious conflict in the region with the possibility that India, Japan, Singapore, South Korea, Russia, and Vietnam, will join the US in containing the Chinese influence. Mearsheimer predicts that, in the future, China will try to be the regional hegemon by attempting to dominate Asia just like the US dominating the Americas. It is possible that, as China gains more and more power, it will try to reduce if not eliminate the American influence in Asia just like what the US has done in the past to push the European powers out of the Western hemisphere. Therefore, it is possible that China will try to promote its own version of the "Monroe Doctrine". Thus, it is certain that, when Beijing has its own "Monroe Doctrine", it will not welcome the perpetual presence of the US maintaining a large military footprint in the Chinese sphere of influence. China will, therefore, seek to push the US military presence out of Asia when it has the capacity to do so.

---

[258] J. Mearsheimer, China's Unpeaceful Rise, *Current History*, April 2006, 160–162.

Mearsheimer argues that the most powerful country will naturally seek to become the regional hegemon and not yield to other competitors. Consequently, he predicts that the US will respond negatively to future Chinese attempts to dominate East Asia. Washington will try its best to maintain its hegemonic role by containing China, decreasing its influence and preventing it from regional dominance. Indeed, the US will respond to China the way it responded to the Soviet Union during the Cold War.

Mearsheimer argues that China's neighbors will be fearful of its rise and will want China to become the regional hegemon. Conceivably, India, Japan, Russia, and possibly Singapore, South Korea and Vietnam, are increasingly worried about the rise of the dragon and are finding ways to shackle it. Therefore, in the future, these countries will align with the US to contain China.

China's grand strategy[259]

Beijing, over the past decade, has become increasingly concerned about the American agenda to contain China. Therefore, the best grand basic strategy of China is to prevent this containment strategy from succeeding. China sees the US as selfishly and hypocritically seeking to perpetuate global and regional hegemony. At present, the global system is unipolar especially in its military and political aspects. Chinese basic policy is to change the unipolar world to a multipolar one by strengthening its relations with the neighboring countries, and creating a buffer zone to prevent the American containment. In recent years, Beijing has emphasized its diplomatic theme which is called "charmed offensive" by adopting flexible policies and even making compromises with the neighbors. Its diplomatic offensive over the past decade has helped to expand Chinese influence and obviate the US containment somewhat. Beijing has been very successful in improving its relations with the Southeast Asian states and South Korea. Indeed, the so-called "China fever" is spreading throughout Southeast Asia.

---

[259] Yong Deng, Hegemon on the Offensive: Chinese Perspectives on U.S. Global Strategy, *Political Science Quarterly*, 116(3), 2001, 343–365.

The latest Chinese overture towards the region is the mantra called "peaceful rise". Beijing often emphasizes that as it prospers, the region will prosper likewise. Chinese prosperity, therefore, will not threaten anyone. As for Southeast Asia, Beijing is placing a higher priority to promote close relationships and lessen the concern on "China threat". Beijing has also wooed the ASEAN countries by offering many tangible rewards or "carrots". The important card played by China is the offer of an FTA (Free Trade Area) with ASEAN in 2001. Moreover, Beijing proposed further areas of cooperation including the 2003 joint declaration between ASEAN and China which makes it the first strategic partner of ASEAN. Overall, Beijing has been very successful, in recent years, to woo ASEAN and lessen its fear of the so-called "China threat".

Even though Beijing has been very successful in building trust with its neighbors, Washington continues to harp on the "China threat" to the region. Even though many countries in the region are less fearful of the so-called "China threat", residual concerns about the rise of China and a potential hegemonic role remain. Indeed, as several countries see the unfolding drama of China's inexorable rise, concerns over "China threat" might well emerge again.

China, US, and Southeast Asia

US grand strategy towards China: containment policy[260]

Simply put, China's rise is instilling fear in the US which views China as the emerging challenger to American hegemony despite an important

---

[260] R. Berstein and R.H. Munro, The Coming Conflict with America, *Foreign Affairs,* 76(2), 1997, 18–32; R.S. Ross, Beijing as a Conservative Power, *Foreign Affairs* 76(2), 1997, 33–43; D.Byman, *et al*, U.S. Policy Options Toward an Emerging China, *Pacific Review,* 12(3), 1999, 421–451; Z.Khalizad, *et al., The United States and a Rising China,* Rand Coperation,1999; T. Donnelly and C. Monaghan, The Bush Doctrine and the Rise of China, *National Security Outlook,* AEI online, April 30, 2007; D. Roy, Rising China and U.S. Interests: Inevitable vs. Contingent Hazards, *Orbis,* winter, 2003, 126–137; J. Tkacik, Hedging Against China, Backgrounder #1925, April 17, 2006, Heritage Foundation.

and mutually beneficial trading relationship. Many hawkish neo-conservatives prominent in the former Bush administration viewed China as a threat and a rising hegemon — first as the regional hegemon in East Asia, and in a long term, a global one.

Not surprisingly, Washington under the former Bush administration concluded that the most appropriate grand strategy towards China must be containment. However, comprehensive containment strategy towards China, like the one used during the Cold War, would be difficult to implement in its entirety because there will be international and domestic opposition against comprehensive containment. Domestic opposition will come from the business sector that trades with and invests in mainland China. Indeed, American consumers do benefit from low-priced, good quality Chinese-made products sold at Wal-Mart. Right now, China has become the third largest trading partner of the US. International opposition will come from countries bordering China which do not want to openly support a confrontational containment policy and become enemies of China. As a result, realistic American strategy towards China has to come in the form of "half containment and half engagement" and produce a hybrid called "congagement". The basic strategy is to pursue military containment and economic engagement.[261] In my view, Southeast Asia and Thailand will probably play a hedging game by remaining friendly to both China and the US and not take sides in US-Sino rivalry. In this regard, I differ from John Mearsheimer's view that India, Japan, Singapore, South Korea, Russia, and Vietnam, will join the US in containing China. Indeed, when great powers collide, the most logical strategy is for the smaller countries including Thailand to stay out of their clash.

China-US economic competition in Southeast Asia[262]

As mentioned, Beijing has been very successful in expanding its influence in Asia especially in the economic dimension. Between 1995

---

[261] Khalizad, Z., *et al*. Op. Cit.

[262] D. R. Dillon and J. Tkacik, China and ASEAN: Endangered American Primacy in Southeast Asia, Backgrounder, #1886, October 19, 2005, *Heritage Foundation*; R. Sutter Asia in the Balance: America and China's 'Peaceful Rise, *Current History* (September 2004), 284–289; E. Economy, Op. Cit.; W. Bert, Op. Cit.; R. Sokolsky *et al.*, *The Role of Southeast Asia in U.S. Strategy Toward China*, Rand, 2003, 29–42.

and 2002, ASEAN–China trade has expanded twenty percent every year. In 2004, trade volume between China and ASEAN increased to almost US$100 billion. Moreover, China promotes an ASEAN–China FTA by 2010. It is predicted that ASEAN-China FTA will eventually have a trade volume valued around US$1.2 trillion.

However, if we compare ASEAN–China trade with ASEAN–Japan trade or ASEAN–US trade, ASEAN–China trade lags behind the Japanese and American trade with ASEAN. Moreover, there are some in the region which still have negative attitudes towards the increase of Chinese economic role in the region; especially since there is widespread fear that cheap Chinese products will flood into regional markets.

However, compared with China, the US seems to be a laggard in the development of FTAs with the Southeast Asian countries with the exception of Singapore. It is still slowly negotiating with Thailand and Malaysia but there is no policy or political will to sign an FTA with ASEAN as a bloc. Moreover, the US never has had a summit with ASEAN.

China–US political and security competition in Southeast Asia[263]

Even though Beijing has been very successful in promoting close economic relations with Southeast Asia, its political and security policies are arguably less successful because the US has upgraded its military ties to this region after September 11. The basic Chinese strategy on security is to woo ASEAN by acceding to the Treaty of Amity and Cooperation in Southeast Asia in 2003. Besides, China has stated its intention to accede to the Southeast Asia Nuclear Weapon Free Zone Treaty too. Beijing has already signed the declaration to peacefully manage the territorial disputes over the Spratlys islands in the South China Sea. And finally, in late 2003, Beijing has signed the joint declaration

---

[263] D. R. Dillon and J. Tkacik, Op. Cit.; R. Sutter, Op. Cit.; E. Economy, Op. Cit.; W. Bert, Op. Cit.; R. Sokolsky *et al.*, Op. Cit.

with ASEAN making the former the first strategic partner of the regional grouping.

Even though the US has neither acceded to the Treaty of Amity and Cooperation in Southeast Asia nor to the Southeast Asia Nuclear Weapon Free Zone Treaty, the superpower has been pursuing its so-called "hub & spoke" strategy by strengthening bilateral military relations with the countries in the region. Since September 11 incident, the former Bush government has declared that Southeast Asia has become the second front on the war on terror, and has used this war as a justification to increase its military role in the region. The US has intensified its military relations with Thailand and the Philippines. In 2003, both countries have received the major non-NATO ally status from Washington. Singapore is also becoming a de facto military ally with the U.S and is negotiating a new agreement on military cooperation with the superpower.

However, despite the intensifying US military presence in the region, there is the perception among many in Muslim-majority countries in Southeast Asia that they do not fully trust the US. Indeed, there is a dramatic rise in anti-American sentiments across the region, particularly after the US invasion and occupation of Iraq. This is viewed by many as an unjust and illegitimate war which undermines the credibility and the legitimacy of the US to be a global leader.

Although China cannot presently challenge American military supremacy in the region by a long shot, the US is increasingly viewed with distrust among the public in the region. Therefore, in the long term, it is possible that the role of China will become more tolerated if not welcomed, especially with the use of its soft power and charmed diplomatic offensive, which will eventually erode American influence in the region.

China–ASEAN Relations

China–ASEAN relations have developed rapidly. This section of the chapter will try to analyze China–ASEAN relations with a focus on Chinese strategy towards ASEAN. It argues that the heart of Chinese strategy is to expand its influence into Southeast Asia and to prevent the US containment of China.[264]

Chinese strategy towards ASEAN

During the cold war, China was an enemy of ASEAN. But relations improved considerably after Vietnam's invasion of Cambodia and subsequently the end of the Cold War. However, in the early 1990s, China was still reluctant to participate in the multilateral forum of ASEAN. China joined the ASEAN Regional Forum in 1994 and gained the full dialogue status with ASEAN in 1996 and the first China–ASEAN summit was held in 1997. However, China has changed its policy from a reactive and defensive stance to a very active and confident one by participating in various multilateral forums.

A milestone in China–ASEAN relations was in 2000 when former Prime Minister Zhu Rongji proposed the idea of China–ASEAN free trade area. In the following year during the ASEAN–China summit, the leaders officially agreed to establish an ASEAN–China FTA.[265] However, some in the regional grouping still see ASEAN–China FTA negatively and suspect that China is merely using the FTA as a strategic tool to improve relations with ASEAN, to lessen their fear of "China threat", and to expand its influence into the region.[266]

---

[264] Kuik Cheng-Chwee, Multilateralism in China's ASEAN Policy: Its Evolution, Characteristics, and Aspiration, *Contemporary Southeast Asia,* Vol 27, No 1, 2005, 102–122.; J. Cheng Sino–ASEAN Relations in the Early Twenty-first Century, *Contemporary Southeast Asia,* 23(3) 2001, 420–451; M. Stuart–Fox Southeast Asia and China: The Role of History and Culture in Shaping Future Relations, *Contemporary Southeast Asia,* 26(1) 2004, 116–139; M. Stuart–Fox, *A Short History of China and Southeast Asia,* Allen & Unwin, 2003: Chapter.10.

[265] Kuik Cheng-Chwee, Op. Cit.

[266] B. Wain, Free trade: Nothing's Free *Far, Eastern Economic Review*, October 31, 2002. Available at www.feer.com; China-ASEAN pact unlikely to be speedy, *Bangkok Post,* September 9, 2002, 6; China seen as rival and friend, *Bangkok Post,* September 14, 2002; M. Vatikiotis and M. Hiebert , Free Trade Agreements: China's Tight Embrace, *Far Eastern Economic Review,* July 17, 2003. Available at www.feer.com; K.G. Cai, The ASEAN-China Free Trade Agreement and East Asian Regional Grouping, *Contemporary Southeast Asia,* 25(3) 2003, 387–404.

But overall, ASEAN has been receptive to the Chinese FTA idea. ASEAN probably realizes that it is inevitable that Beijing will rise to be the major power in the region. The Chinese Mainland attracts a lot of direct investment and its rate of economic growth is the highest in the world. Therefore, it is rational for ASEAN to harness the economic rise of China and accept its FTA overtures to gain more economic and other benefits.

In 2002, Beijing further activated its active policy towards ASEAN including the signing of a framework agreement for FTA which identified areas of cooperation including agriculture and non-traditional security issues. Beijing also acceded to the Treaty of Amity and Cooperation in Southeast Asia and stated its intention to accede to the Southeast Asian Nuclear Weapon Free Zone Treaty. China also signed the declaration with ASEAN concerning the peaceful management of the Spratlys territorial dispute in the South China Sea. The latest development concerning Chinese pro-active diplomacy towards ASEAN is the signing of the join declaration on strategic partners making China becoming the first strategic partner of ASEAN. China is also the first country that has FTA with ASEAN.

Another Chinese pro-active strategy is its active role in the ASEAN+3 (APT). Presumably, Beijing realized that if the APT could develop and evolve into an East Asia Community that would provide another opportunity for China to expand its leadership role and even dominate these multilateral processes in the long run. Especially attractive to Beijing in the APT is the absence of its US superpower rival.

ASEAN strategy towards China

ASEAN seems to accept the apparent inevitability of China's rise by positively respond to Chinese diplomatic overtures. However, ASEAN countries are still worried and uneasy concerning the future intent and the impact of China — geopolitically and economically.[267] In the economic

---

[267] Yong Deng, Managing China's Hegemonic Ascension: Engagement from Southeast Asia, *The Journal of Strategic Studies,* 21(1), 1998, 21–43.; W. Bert, Op. Cit., 175–209.

dimension, China will rise to become a leader which might impact negatively on ASEAN economies, since China is still being perceived as the economic competitor of ASEAN by producing the same products, competing in the same markets, and competing for the same FDI.

On China-ASEAN FTA, some ASEAN analysts see that, eventually, ASEAN will gain much from this FTA. On the contrary, this FTA might impact negatively on ASEAN since free trade with the Chinese Mainland will mean allowing cheap Chinese products to swamp ASEAN markets. Moreover, ASEAN-China FTA might divert and accelerate more FDI to China and less into ASEAN. Some in ASEAN argue that Beijing's hidden agenda is the geopolitical strategy of using economic FTA diplomacy as a tool to expand its influence into Southeast Asia.[268]

Therefore, the ASEAN grand strategy towards China is to bandwagon or get closer to China economically, but at the same time, ASEAN is also playing a balancing game, by trying to prevent the Chinese geo-political domination of the region.[269] The main strategy is the traditional balance of power strategy, by drawing in other major powers to balance China.[270] That is why ASEAN has tried to strengthen its relations with and bring in Japan, India, Australia, and the US to counter balance Chinese influence. One indicator includes ASEAN's FTAs with Japan, India and Australia. At the same time, these powers appear to share a mutual interest with ASEAN — the desire to avoid Chinese hegemony in the region. And India appears to have the heft to balance China.

The rise of India

Comparing the rise of China and India

China and India have the largest demography in the world. The former has around 1.3 billion people; the latter has about 1 billion. Due to its

---

[268] B. Wain, Op. Cit., China–ASEAN pact unlikely to be speedy, *Bangkok Post,* Op. Cit.; China seen as rival and friend, *Bangkok Post,* Op. Cit.; M. Vatikiotis and M. Hiebert Op. Cit.; K.G. Cai, Op. Cit.

[269] D. Roy Southeast Asia and China: Balancing or Bandwagoning?, *Contemporary Southeast Asia,* 27(2), 2005, 305–322.

[270] Lee Kuan Yew, Need for a Balancer on East Asia's Way to World Eminence, *International Herald Tribune.* Available at www.iht.com.

higher rate of population growth, India will eventually become number one demographically, which would provide a large, cheap and young labor force for India's economic development.[271]

The Indian economy in 2000 was much smaller than the Chinese but its rate of growth is very high. It is not inconceivable that if India were to maintain its 10 percent growth rate for the next few decades, it will eventually catch up with China. According to the projections of one study, the size of Indian economy will equal the Chinese by 2050. That would make both countries becoming the largest economies in the world.[272] Moreover, India and China are developing their technologies very fast, and in the mid-term, both might be able catch up with the US in some technological sectors.[273]

Chindia?

The word "Chindia" is derived from the combination of the two words "China" and "India". Chindia reflects the idea that India and China are rising and it is possible that they will cooperate. Their relations will be positive.[274] India and China are among the countries registering the highest economic growth rates in the world. And their populations combined would comprise one third of the globe's population. According to the Chindia theory, the strengths of both countries are complementary. China is strong on industry, merchandise goods, and infrastructure, whereas India is strong on service sector and information technology. Simply put, China is strong on hardware, whereas India is strong on software. In 2006, Prime Minister Wen Jia Bao, declared that India and China will become the source of power in the 21st century and Sino–India cooperation will be like two pagodas: one on hardware and the other on software. Is Chindia a fact or fiction? Conceivably, if the US were to face relative decline and retrenchment in Asia in the aftermath

---

[271] Kugler, Op. Cit.

[272] Ibid.; see also India years away from matching China's role, *Bangkok Post*, May 5, 2004, 2.

[273] China, India ready to challenge US, *Bangkok Post*, February 26, 2005, B2.

[274] S. MacDonald, China and India: Same Globalization Road, Different Destinies, *Yaleglobal*, October 24, 2007.

of its costly misadventures in Iraq and Afghanistan and weakened by the 2007–09 American Financial Crisis triggered by its sub-prime mortgage problems, Chinadia might well become a new condominium which lay the rules of the game in East and South Asia. However, I argue that Chindia is more a fiction than a fact and that China and India will face greater competition than cooperation in economics, geopolitics and military affairs. Even in the wake of a relative decline of US power, Japan, Russia, ASEAN and Australia cannot accept a Chindia condominium which lays down the law for others.

Economic competition

The Chindia theory, which sees two economies complementing each other, is not convincing because there is no simplistic division of labor with the Chinese focusing primarily on hardware while the Indians on software only. This is because China is now trying to develop its software sector and its service sectors to compete with India and other countries. At the same time, India is also trying to develop its hardware sector and its industry to compete with China and other countries. India has several industrial conglomerates such Tata company in the auto sector, Vedanta and Hindalco companies in the steel industry. Moreover, Indian pharmaceutical companies are developing at a fast pace.[275] In addition, both the Indian and Chinese economic engines have an insatiable demand for considerable energy and natural resources. It is not unthinkable that in the years ahead, both emerging giant economies will be competing more intensely for limited natural resources. Already companies from both countries are seriously competing to win bids in the exploration of natural gas and oil.

Geopolitical competition

Geopolitically, both India and China view each other as real and potential rivals. Both countries have a long history of conflict with each other.

---

[275] Ibid.; see also J. Malik, India and China: Bound to Collide? in P.R. Kumaraswamy (ed.) *Security Beyond Survival: Essay for K. Subrahmanyam,* Sage Publications, New Delhi, 2004, 127–165.; B. Chellaney, Assessing India's Reactions to China's Peaceful Development Doctrine, *NBR Analysis,* 18(5), April 2008.

In 1962, both countries fought a war over their disputed Himalayas borders. India accused China of invading and occupying some parts of Indian Kashmir. In 1998, when India successfully tested its nuclear weapons, then Foreign Minister Fernandez argued that the fundamental objective of possessing nuclear weapons was to deter China. India is also concerned about close China-Pakistan relations. China plays a very important role in the development of nuclear weapons by Pakistan. And China is also helping Pakistan develop deep sea ports. China is also strengthening its security ties with neighboring countries of India, especially, with Burma and Bangladesh.[276] India is also warming up to the US. In 2006, former President George W. Bush visited India for the first time and announced a strategic partnership with India. It can be interpreted that the objective of closer US-India cooperation is to contain China.[277]

Military competition

China's increase of its military capability is very alarming for India. Beijing's military budget has increased more than 10 percent for almost 20 years. In 2007, it amounted to US$40 billion, a whopping increase of 18 percent. India has responded by increasing its military capability to compete with China. Indian naval force is very powerful, now, ranking number three in the world. India emphasizes naval domination in the Indian Ocean. However, naval competition in the Indian Ocean between China and India will become more intense in the future. Both China and India depend on oil transportation from the Middle East through the Indian Ocean. As a result, both are developing their naval forces to protect their oil routes in the Indian Ocean.[278]

Sino–Indian competition in Southeast Asia

Both China and India would like to expand their influences to Southeast Asia. But China has advantages over India. China has intensified its

---

[276] Malik, Op. Cit.

[277] C. Mohan, India and the Balance of Power, *Foreign Affairs,* 85(4), 2006, 17–32.

[278] Malik, Op. Cit.

relations with ASEAN countries. In 2001, China and ASEAN agreed to set up ASEAN–China FTA. Later on, they signed joint declaration on strategic partnership. China has summit meetings with ASEAN since 1997. China also cooperates with ASEAN within the ASEAN+3 framework.

Hitherto, India in ASEAN could not compete with China for influence in ASEAN. However, in recent years, India has come up with its pro-active policy to compete with China. India has its first summit with ASEAN in 2002 and in 2003 has agreed to set up FTA with ASEAN. Moreover, India is attempting to get involved in the East Asia Cooperation, first by proposing to expand ASEAN+3 to be ASEAN+4. Indian basic position is that it does not want to see the setting up of East Asia Community with only 13 countries (ASEAN, China, Japan, and Korea). India does not want China to dominate ASEAN+3 and East Asia Community. As a result, India is pursuing very hard to be part of the East Asia Community to balance and hedge against Chinese influence. India finally succeeded by becoming a member of the East Asia Summit or ASEAN+6, which includes not only ASEAN+3 countries but also India, Australia, and New Zealand.[279]

To conclude in this section, it has become increasingly clear that Southeast Asia has been, and will be, in the future, the battleground for big power competition, playing the game of trying to exert their influences, their hegemonies, and balancing each other: the classic balance of power game.

Conclusion

Thailand has a geostrategic culture which adapts and accommodates the waxing and waning of great powers. Its relations with the great powers — the US, China and India — are no exceptions. Rather than viewing China and India as long term security threats, the Thais will pragmatically seek to get along with the two Asian giants and even to

---

[279] S. Limaye, India's Relations with Southeast Asia Take a Wing, *Southeast Asian Affairs,* 2003, 39–51; V. Sahni, India and the Asian Security Architecture, *Current History,* April 2006, 163–168.

profit from good relations with them. Although Thai society and interest groups have become more pluralistic, complex and diverse, there are no sharp differences of domestic opinions towards the proposition that the rise of China and India is to be accommodated if not welcomed. In the meantime, Bangkok hedges its bets by keeping good ties with Washington.

Indeed the "enemy" to Thailand today is neither China nor India but within. Since the military *coup de tat* against democratically elected Prime Minister Thaksin in September 2006, Thailand has been mired in domestic political conflict and street protests. Thaksin's allies reconstituted themselves under new ruling parties and the subsequent Prime Ministers Samak Sundaravej and Somchai Wongsawat were Thaksin's proxies even while the latter was in exile. Things came to a head when the anti-Thaksin People's Alliance for Democracy (a proxy for royalists, the military and the Bangkok elite and middle class) stormed the Savarnabhumi International Airport, the busiest air hub of Southeast Asia, and paralyzed its operations late 2008. Abhisit Vejjajiva, leader of the opposition Democrat Party, then became Prime Minister in December 2008.

At the time of writing, it is uncertain whether the change of ruling parties will usher a new era of domestic peace or merely an interlude to greater domestic violence between the yellow forces of the anti-Thaksin PAD and the red forces of pro-Thaksin elements (with strong support from the rural sectors). Arguably, the greatest "threat" to Thailand today is political instability and an escalation of political violence due to a lack of national consensus on the rules of the political game.

Besides the damage to its important tourist industry, the domestic political conflict also resulted in the postponement of the ASEAN Summit in Thailand from 2008 to the following year. In this regard, this postponement made ASEAN looked bad in the eyes of the world. A global financial crisis was raging and the leaders of ASEAN could not even meet — thanks to Thai domestic politics. Moreover, it is imperative that ASEAN must remain cohesive and credible against the backdrop of a rising China and India. Thailand and ASEAN must live with the reality of rising regional powers and the onus is on them whether they are shrewd enough to become the beneficiaries and not pawns of ascending powers.

Bibliography

Abe, Junichi, *Chuugoku to Higashi Ajia no Anzenhosho* (*China and Security in East Asia*), Tokyo, Meitoku Shuppansha, 2006, pp. 192–194.

AFP, China's Yellow Sand Hits Japan and South Korea, 3 March 2008 in AFP website. Available at http://dsc.discovery.com/news/2008/03/03/japan-desert-sand.html.

Ahmn, Soon-Bum, China as Number One, *Current History* (September 2001), unpaginated.

Amin, Samir, India, a Great Power, *Monthly Review*, 56(9), 2005, 6–7.

Anderson, Kym, *Changing Comparative Advantages in China: Effects on Food, Feed and Fibre Markets* (Paris: OECD Development Studies), 1990.

Ang, Cheng Guan, Michael Leifer on Cambodia and the Third Indochina Conflict, in *Order and Security in Southeast Asia Essays in Memory of Michael Leifer*, Joseph Chinyong Liow and Ralf Emmers (eds.), Great Britain, Routledge, 2006, pp. 161–174.

AP, U.S. diplomat says China's influence in Southeast Asia is unproductive, 27 July 2007, in The Associated Press/KI-Media website [downloaded on 18 August 2008]. Available at http://ki-media.blogspot.com/2007/07/us-diplomat-china-is-source-of.html.

Archaya, Amitav, Do norms and identity matter? Community and power in Southeast Asia's regional order, in *Order and Security in Southeast Asia Essays in Memory of Michael Leifer*, Joseph Chinyong Liow and Ralf Emmers (eds.), Great Britain, Routledge, 2006, pp. 78–92.

Baginda, Abdul Razak, Malaysian Perceptions of China: From Hostility to Cordiality, in Herbert Yee and Ian Storey (eds.), *The China Threat: Perceptions, Myths and Reality*, London, RoutledgeCurzon, 2002, 227–247.

Bakshian, Douglas, Chinese Premier Ends Philippine Visit, After Signing Billions of Dollars in Projects, 16 January 2007 in the Voice of America

News Com website [downloaded on 1 November 2007]. Available at http://www.voanews.com/tibetan/archive/2007-01/2007-01-16-voa2.cfm.

Bangkok Post, China-ASEAN pact unlikely to be speedy, 9 September 2002, *Bangkok Post*: 6.

Bangkok Post, China, India ready to challenge US, 26 Feb 2005, *Bangkok Post*: B2.

Bangkok Post, China overtakes US as biggest consumer, 18 Feb 2005, *Bangkok Post*: B7.

Bangkok Post, China replacing US as world's leading consumer, 6 March 2005, *Bangkok Post*: 5.

Bangkok Post, India years away from matching China's role, 5 May 2004, *Bangkok Post*: 2.

Bangkok Post, US losing its scientific edge, 4 May 2005, *Bangkok Post*: 7.

Berlin, Donald, SPEAKING FREELY — The emerging Bay of Bengal, 25 Jan 2005 in the Atimes website [downloaded on 11 March 2006]. Available at http://www.atimes.com/atimes/South_Asia/GA25Df05.html

Berstein, R. and R. H. Munro, The Coming Conflict with America, *Foreign Affairs*, 76(2) 1997, 18–32.

Bert, W., *The United States, China and Southeast Asian Security*, Palgrave Macmillan, 2003.

Brzezinski, Z., *Grand Chessboard*, New York, Basic Books, 1997.

Byman, D., *et al.*, U.S. Policy Options Toward an Emerging China, *Pacific Review*, 12(3), 1999, 421–451.

Cai, K. G., The ASEAN–China Free Trade Agreement and East Asian Regional Grouping, *Contemporary Southeast Asia*, 25(3), 2003, 387–404.

Calder, Kent, Higashi Ajianiokeru Chiikishugi to Doumei (Regionalism and Alliance in East Asia), Chapter 4 in Tokai Daigaku Heiwa Senryaku Kokusai Kenkyujo (ed.), Higashi Ajia ni Kyodotai ha Dekiruka (Is it possible to establish a community in East Asia?), Japan: Shakaihyoronsha, 2006, 82.

Chan, G., *China's Compliance in Global Affairs*, New Jersey and London, World Scientific, 2006.

Chandrasekhar, C. P. and Jayati Ghosh, Rising Inequality in China, 3 January 2006, in *The Hindu*, 2006.

Channelnewsasia, Indian PM says nuclear deal to bring new status 28 September 2008 in Channelnewsasia [downloaded on 29 September 2008]. Available at http://www.channelnewsasia.com/stories/afp_asiapacirfic/print/378938/1/.html.

Chellaney, B., Assessing India's Reactions to China's Peaceful Development Doctrine, in *NBR Analysis*, 18(5), April 2008.

Chen, King C. (ed.) *China and the Three Worlds*, New York, M E Sharpe Inc, 1978.

Cheng, J., Sino–ASEAN Relations in the Early Twenty-first Century, *Contemporary Southeast Asia*, 23(3) 2001, 420–451.

Chicago Council on Global Affairs, *World Public Opinion 2007: Globalization and Trade, Climate Change, Genocide and Darfur, Future of the United Nations, US Leadership, Rise of China* (Country Highlights: Philippines), 2007.

Chin, Kin Wah, The foreign policy of Singapore, in *Order and Security in Southeast Asia Essays in Memory of Michael Leifer*, Joseph Chinyong Liow and Ralf Emmers (eds.), Great Britain: Routledge, 2006, pp. 196–211.

China Daily, Trade between Philippines, Chinese mainland hits record high, 25 January 2008, Xinhua, China Daily website [downloaded on 2 November 2008]. Available at http://www.chinadaily.com.cn/bizchina/2008-01/25/content_6421890.htm.

Chong, Alan, Singapore's foreign policy beliefs as 'Abridged Realism': Pragmatic and liberal prefixes in the foreign policy thought of Rajaratnam, Lee, Koh, and Mahbubani, in *International Relations of the Asia-Pacific*, 6(2) Japan, Oxford Journal, 2006, pp. 269–306.

Christoffersen, Gaye, China and the Asia-Pacific, *Asian Survey*, 36(11), November 1996, unpaginated.

Chua, Amy, *Day of Empire: How Hyperpowers Rise to Global Dominance — And Why They Fall*, New York, Doubleday, 2007.

DB, Alice, China and ASEAN: Renavigating Relations for a 21st Century Asia, *Asian Survey*, 42(4), July–August 2003, 622–647.

Deng, Yong, Hegemon on the Offensive: Chinese Perspectives on U.S. Global Strategy, *Political Science Quarterly*, 116(3), 2001, 343–365.

Deng, Yong, Managing China's Hegemonic Ascension: Engagement from Southeast Asia, *The Journal of Strategic Studies*, 21(8), 1998, 21–43.

Dillon, D. R. and J. Tkacik, China and ASEAN: Endangered American Primacy in Southeast Asia in *Heritage Foundation* Backgrounder #1886, October 19, 2005.

Donnelly, T. and C. Monaghan, The Bush Doctrine and the Rise of China, *National Security Outlook* AEI online, April 30, 2007.

E. Economy, China's Rise in Southeast Asia: Implications for Japan and the United States, in *Council on Foreign Relations*. Available at www.cfr.org.

Economic Development Board (EDB), Global Partnership, 1 Aug 2005 in the EDB website [downloaded on 10 March 2006]. Available at http://www.sedb.com/edb/sg/en_uk/index/news_room/publications/singapore_investment/singapore_invesdtment8/global_partnership_.html.

Economist, Special report on China and its region, 31 March 2007 in *Economist*, unpaginated.

Embassy of the Philippines India, Philippine–India Relations: An Overview, in the Embassy of the Philippines, New Delhi, India website [downloaded on 2 November 2008]. Available at http://www.newdelhipe.com/philippines-india-relation.html.

Emerson, Donald, Shocks of recognition: Leifer, realism, and regionalism in Southeast Asia, in *Order and Security in Southeast Asia Essays in Memory of Michael Leifer*, Joseph Chinyong Liow and Ralf Emmers (eds.), Great Britain: Routledge, 2006, pp. 10–28.

Feng, Yongping, The peaceful transition of power from the UK to the US, *The Chinese Journal of International Politics*, 1(1), 2006, 83–108.

Ferguson, Niall, *Colossus: The Price of America's Empire*, New York, Penguin, 2004.

Finlay, Christopher and Andrew Watson, Economic growth and trade dependency in China, in *China Rising: Nationalism and Interdependence*, David S. G. Goodman and Gerald Segal (eds.), London and New York, Routledge, 1997.

Fujimaki, Yuichi, Higashi Ajia ni Okeru Enerugi Anzenhosho (Energy Security in East Asia), in *Higashi Ajia ni Kyodotai ha* Dekiruka, p. 171.

Fullbrook, David, China's growing influence in Cambodia, 6 October 2006 in *The Asia Times Online* [downloaded on 18 August 2008]. Available at http://www.atimes.com/atimes/Southeast_Asia/HJ06Ae01.html.

Gaulier, Guillaume Gaulier Francoise Lemoine and Deniz Unal-Kesenci, China's emergence and the reorganization of trade flows in Asia, in *China Economic Review*, 18, 2007, 209–243,

George, Susan, *A Fate Worse than Debt: The World Financial Crisis and the Poor*, New York, Grove Weidenfeld, 1990.

Ghosh, Jayati, China and India: The Big Differences, 24 August 2005 in macroscan website. Available at http://www.macroscan.org/cur/aug05/cur240805China_India.htm.

Gilpin, Robert, *Global Political Economy: Understanding the International Economic* Order, Princeton and Oxford, Princeton University Press, 2001.

Goh, Chok Tong, Keynote Address by Prime Minister, Mr Goh Chok Tong, to the Asia Society Conference, on Thursday, 13 May 1993, at 9.00 am at the Hotel Okura, Tokyo Geopolitics in Asia in the Singapore Government Press Release No. 15/May 02-1/93/05/13.

Goodman, David S. G. and Gerald Segal (eds.), *China Rising: Nationalism and Interdependence*, London and New York, Routledge, 1997.

Goodman, Peter S. and Peter Finn, Corruption Stains Timber Trade, 1 April 2007 in *Washington Post* [downloaded on 18 August 2008]. Available at http://www.washingtonpost.com/wp-dyn/content/article/2007/03/31/AR2007033101287.html, p. A01.

Gyngell, Allan, Looking Outwards: ASEAN's External Relations, in Alison Broinowski (ed.), *Understanding ASEAN*, London: Macmillian, 1982.

Haacke, Jurgen, *ASEAN's Diplomatic and Security Culture*, London and NY, Routledge, 2005.

Haacke, Jurgen, Michael Leifer, the balance of power and international relations theory, in *Order and Security in Southeast Asia Essays in Memory of Michael Leifer*, Joseph Chinyong Liow and Ralf Emmers (eds.), Great Britain, Routledge, 2006, pp. 46–60.

Hiratsuka, Daisuke, *Higashi Ajia no Chosen (The Challenge of East Asia)*, Tokyo, Ajia Keizai Kenkyujo, 2006, 8–9.

Hiroshi, Ando, EANET: Higashi Ajia no Senkuteki Rentai (EANET: A Leading Example of Regional Cooperation toward the East Asian Community), in *Higashi Ajia ni Kyodotai ha Dekiruka*, p. 185.

Ho, Abigail, RP-China-Vietnam exploration deal in Spratlys lapses, 11 July 2008, *Philippine Daily Inquirer* online website [downloaded on 11 July 2008]. Available at http://newsinfo.inquirer.net/inquirerheadlines/nation/view/20080711-147739/RP-China-Vietnam-exploration-deal-on-Spratlys-lapses.

Huntington, Samuel P., The Clash of Civilizations, *Foreign Affairs,* 72(3), 1993, 22–49.

Ikenberry, G. John, *The Rise of China and the Future of the West, Foreign Affairs*, January/February, 2008.

India Brand Equity Foundation (IBEF), India Looks East Hits the Road, Nov 2004 in the IBEF website [downloaded on 8 March 2006]. Available at www.ibef.org, p. 4.

India Brand Equity Foundation (IBEF), Look East, Look West: A Bridge Across Asia, November 2004 in the IBEF website [downloaded on 8 March 2006]. Available at www.ibef.org.

India, Directorate General of Commercial Intelligence and Statistics, Ministry of Commerce and Industry, *Provisional Monthly Foreign Trade Data, 2008* in the DGCISKOL website. Available at http://www.dgciskol.nic.in/.

India, Ministry of Commerce and Industry, *India's Share in World Trade*, 27, 2008 in the NICndia website. Available at http://commerce.nic.in/PressRelease/pressrelease_detail.asp?id=540.

India, Ministry of Defence, *Annual Report 2004–05*, New Delhi, Ministry of Defence, 2005.

India, Ministry of External Affairs, *Annual Report 2007–2008*, New Delhi, MEA, 2008.

India, Ministry of External Affairs, *Foreign Affairs Record*, 45(5), 1998; India, Ministry of Defence *Annual Report 1998–1999*, New Delhi, Ministry of Defence, 1999.

India, Ministry of External Affairs, PM'S address at the India–China Economic, Trade and Investment Summit, 14 January 2008 in the Ministry of External Affairs website. Available at http://meaindia.nic.in/.

India, Ministry of Finance, *Economic Survey 1991–92*, New Delhi, Ministry of Finance, 1992.

India, Prime Minister's Office, *Economic Outlook for 2008/09*, New Delhi, Economic Advisory Council to the Prime Minister of India, 2008. Available at http://www.pmindia.nic.in/eac_report_08.pdf.

Jalan, Bimal, *India's Economic Crisis — The Way Ahead*, New Delhi, Oxford University Press, 1991.

Jeshurun, Chandran, *Malaysia: Fifty Years of Diplomacy 1957–2007*, Kuala Lumpur, The Other Press, 2007.

Johnston, Iain and Robert S. Ross (eds.), *Engaging China: The Management of an Emerging Power*, London and New York, Routledge, 1999.

Kagan, Robert, What China Knows that We don't, *The Weekly Standard*, 20 January 1997.

Keohane, Robert O. and Joseph S. Nye Jr., *Power and Interdependence*, Boston, Little, Brown and Company, 1977.

Khalizad, Z., *et al.*, *The United States and a Rising China*, US, Rand Cooperation, 1999.

Koh, Tommy, ASEAN at 40: Perception and Reality, in the US Korea Council website [downloaded on 2 June 2008]. Available at www.uskoreacouncil.org/.../ASEANat40PerceptionandReality.doc.

Koh, Tommy, Asian Values Reconsidered, in *Asia and Europe Essays and Speeches by Tommy Koh*, Yeo Lay Hwee and Asad Latif (eds.), Singapore, Asia Europe Foundation, 2000.

Koh, Tommy, Eight Lessons on Negotiations, in *The Little Red Dot*, Tommy, Koh and Chang Li Lin (eds.), Singapore, World Scientific and IPS, 2005, pp. 199–205.

Koh, Tommy, Southeast Asia, in *America's Role in Asia Asian Views*, San Francisco, Asia Foundation, 2004, pp. 35–54.

Koh, Tommy, *The Quest for World Order Perspectives of a Pragmatic Idealist*, Singapore, Federal Publications, 1998.

Koh, Tommy, *The United States and East Asia*, Singapore, Times Academic Press, 1995.

Koh, Tommy, Rodolfo Severino and Jusuf Wanadi, China and ASEAN: Roadmap to Future, 14 December 2005 *The Business Times* [downloaded on 1 June 2008]. Available at www.ips.org.sg.

Koh, Tommy, What Can East Asia Learn from the European Union, in *Asia and Europe Essays and Speeches by Tommy Koh*, Yeo Lay Hwee and Asad Latif (eds.), Singapore, Asia Europe Foundation, 2000, pp. 59–66.

Koide, Minoru, Nichi Ei Domei Shuryo Katei no Kenkyu (An Analysis on the Termination Process of the Anglo-Japanese Alliance), The Memorial Journal of the 25th Anniversary of Soka University (December 1995), 1224–1232.

Koide, Minoru, The East Asian Community: An Unattainable Dream? *Sodai Heiwa Kenkyu* (Soka University Peace Research), Vols. 22 & 23 (March 2002), 69–81.

Koide, Minoru, Whither Our Region? A Comparative Analysis on the Asia Pacific and East Asia, in *Sodai Heiwa Kenkyu*, the Special Issue on the East Asian Community (March 2005), 59–74.

Kornberg, Judith F. and John R. Faust, *China in World Politics: Polices, Processes, Prospects*, London, Lynne Rienner, 2005, 251.

Kristof, Nicholas D., The Rise of China, *Foreign Affairs*, 72(5), November–December 1993, 59–74.

Kugler, J., *et al.*, Power Transitions and Alliances in the 21st Century, *Asian Perspective*, 25(3), 2001, 5–29.

Kuik, Cheng-Chwee, Multilateralism in China's ASEAN Policy: Its Evolution, Characteristics, and Aspiration, *Contemporary Southeast Asia*, 27(1), 2005, 102–122.

Latif, Asad, *Between Rising Powers: China, Singapore and India*, Singapore, Institute of Southeast Asian Studies, 2007.

Leifer, Michael, ASEAN's Search for Regional Order Faculty Lecture 12, Singapore: Graham Brash, 1987.

Leifer, Michael, China in Southeast Asia: Interdependence and Accommodation, in *Michael Leifer: Selected Works on Southeast Asia*, Chin Kin Wah and Leo Suraydinata (eds.), Singapore, ISEAS, 2005, pp. 258–271.

Leifer, Michael, *Selected Works on Southeast Asia*, Chin Kin Wah and Leo Suryadinata (eds.), Singapore, Institute of Southeast Asian Studies, 2005.

Leifer, Michael, *Singapore's Foreign Policy*, Great Britain: Routledge, 2000.

Leifer, Michael, Taiwan and Southeast Asia, in *Michael Leifer: Selected Works on Southeast Asia*, Chin Kin Wah and Leo Suraydinata (eds.), Singapore, ISEAS, 2005, pp. 272–281.

Leifer, Michael, The ASEAN Peace Process: A Category Mistake, in *Michael Leifer: Selected Works on Southeast Asia*, Chin Kin Wah and Leo Suraydinata (eds.), Singapore, ISEAS, 2005, pp. 119–135.

Leifer, Michael, The Balance of Power and Regional Order, in *The Balance of Power in East Asia*, Michael Leifer (ed.), HK, Royal United Services Institute, 1986, pp. 143–154.

Leifer, Michael, The Role and Paradox of ASEAN, in *The Balance of Power in East Asia* Michael Leifer (eds.), HK, Royal United Services Institute, 1986, pp. 119–131.

Lundhold, Gideon, Pipeline Politics: India and Myanmar, 10 September 2007 in the PINR (Power and Interest News Report) website [downloaded on 18 August 2008]. Available at http://www.pinr.com/report.php?ac=view_report&report_id=679&language_id=1.

Lim, Wha Shin, Higashi Ajia Keizaiken no Kosatsu (An Analysis on the East Asian Economic Zone), in *Higashi Ajia ni Kyodotai ha Dekiruka*: p. 138.

Limaye, S., India's Relations with Southeast Asia Take a Wing, in *Southeast Asian Affairs* 2003, 39–51.

Mahbubani, Kishore, *Beyond the Age of Innocence*, New York, Public Affairs, 2005.

Mahbubani, Kishore, *Can Asians Think?*, Singapore, Times Media, 2002.

Mahbubani, Kishore, Singapore in the United Nations Security Council, in *The Little Red Dot*, Tommy Koh and Chang Li Lin (eds.), Singapore, World Scientific and IPS, 2005, pp. 91–96.

Mahbubani, Kishore, *The New Asian Hemisphere*, New York, Public Affairs, 2008.

Malik, J., India and China: Bound to Collide?, in Kumaraswamy, P. R. (ed.), *Security Beyond Survival: Essay for K. Subrahmanyam*, Sage Publications, New Delhi, 2004, pp. 127–165.

Mallik, Nandita, India A Powerhouse: ASEAN, 13 December 2005 [downloaded on 11 March 2006]. Available at http://www.rediff.com/money/2005/dec/13asean2.htm.

McCartan, Brian, Myanmar deal right neighborly of India, 11 January 2008 in the Asia Times Online website [downloaded on 18 August 2008]. Available at http://www.atimes.com/atimes/Southeast_Asia/JA11Ae01.html.

Mearsheimer, J., China's Unpeaceful Rise, *Current History*, April 2006, 160–162.

METI, The Japanese-Indian Common Study report, June 2006 in the METI website. Available at http://www.meti.go.jp/policy/trade_policy/epa/data/jinEPA_report_j.pdf.

Ministry of Foreign Affairs (MFA), Transcript of Remarks on Malaysia–Singapore Relations by Minister for Foreign Affairs, Prof S Jayakumar in Parliament, 16 May 2002, 16 May 2002 [downloaded on 15 September 2008]. Available at http://app-stg1.mfa.gov.sg/2006/lowres/press/view_press.asp?post_id=1262.

Mochizuki, Mike, U.S.-Japan Relations in the Asia-Pacific Region, Chapter 1 in Akira Iriye and Robert A. Wampler (eds.), *Partnership: The United States and Japan 1951–2001*, Tokyo, Kodansha International, 2001, 29–31.

Mohamad, Mahathir and Shintaro Ishihara, *The Voice of Asia: Two Leaders Discuss the Coming Century*, Tokyo, Kodansah International, 1995.

Mohan, Malik J., South Asia in China's Foreign Relations, *Pacifica Review*, 13(1), February, 2001, 80.

Myrdal, Karl Gunnar, *Asian Drama: An Inquiry into the Poverty of Nations, 3 Vols.*, New York, Pantheon Books, 1968.

Nishiguchi, Kiyoshi (ed.), Higashi Ajia Kyodotai no Kouchiku (The Building of the East Asian Community), Tokyo, Mineruba Shobo, 2006.

Nye, Joseph S. Jr., *Soft Power: The Means to Success in World Politics*, New York, Public Affairs, 2004, translated by Yamaoka Yoichi as *Sofuto Pawa*, Tokyo, Nihonkeizai Shimbunsha, 2004, 142–144.

Ollier, Peter, Philippines plans to follow India in limiting patentability, 6 May 2008 in the Managing Intellectual Property website [downloaded on 2 November 2008]. Available at http://www.managingip.com/Article/1927492/Philippines-plans-to-follow-India-in-limiting-patentability.html.

Patnaik, Prabhat, International Capital and National Economic Policy: A Critique of India's Economic Reforms, *Economic and Political Weekly*, 29(12), 1994, 683–690.

People's Republic of China, Ministry of Foreign Affairs, China–US Relations in the New Century, Speech by Foreign Minister Yang Jiechi at the Luncheon Marking the Inauguration of the Kissinger Institute on China and the United States at the Wilson Center, 30 July 2008 in the FMRPC website. Available at http://www.fmprc.gov.cn/eng/wjdt/zyjh/t461226.htm.

People's Republic of China, Ministry of Foreign Affairs, President Hu Jintao's Speech at the Meeting between the Leaders of G8 and Developing Nations, 9 July 2008. Available at http://www.fmprc.gov.cn/eng/wjdt/zyjh/t455676.htm.

People's Republic of China, Ministry of Foreign Affairs, Remarks by Hu Jintao President of the People's Republic of China at Collective Meeting of

Leaders of Five Developing Countries, Japan, 8 July 2008. Available at http://www.fmprc.gov.cn/eng/wjdt/zyjh/t455737.htm.

Perkovich, George, Is India a Major Power, The *Washington Quarterly*, 27(1), Winter (2003–04), 129–144.

Pulta, Benjamin B., RP risks war with China on Spratlys baseline bill, 24 April 2008, in *The Daily Tribune* online [downloaded on 2 November 2008]. Available at http://www.tribune.net.ph/20080424/headlines/20080424hed1.html.

Radio Free Asia, China's Growing Presence in Cambodia, 5 May 2008 [downloaded on 18 August 2008]. Available at http://www.rfa.org/english/news/cambodia/cambodia_china-05232008092653.html.

Ravallion, Martin and Gaurav Datt, Why Has Economic Growth Been More Pro-Poor in Some States of India than Others, *Journal of Development Economics*, 68, (2002), 381–444. Available at http://poverty.worldbank.org/files/13995_JDE2002.pdf.

Research and Information System for Developing Countries (RIS), Seminar on Emerging East Asian Regionalism Options for India Feb 10, 2005, in the RIS website [downloaded on 8 march 2006]. Available at www.ris.org.in/Seminar%20on%20Emerging%20East%20Asian%20Regionalism.pdf.

Ross, R. S., Beijing as a Conservative Power, *Foreign Affairs*, 76(2), 1997, 33–43.

Ross, Robert S., China and the Stability of East Asia, in Robert S. Ross (ed.), *East Asia in Transition*, Armonk, N.Y., M.E. Sharpe, 1995.

Roy, D., Rising China and U.S. Interests: Inevitable vs. Contingent Hazards, *Orbis* 2003, 126–137.

Roy, D., Southeast Asia and China: Balancing or Bandwagoning?, *Contemporary Southeast Asia*, 27(2), 2005, 305–322.

Rufo, Aries, Chinese Money Meets Filipino Politics, 11 October 2007 in the Asia Sentinel Consulting website 11 October 2007 [downloaded on 27 october 2008]. Available at http://www.asiasentinel.com/index.php?Itemid=31&id=758&option=com_content&task=view.

Sahni, V, India and the Asian Security Architecture, *Current History*, April 2006, 163–168.

Saravanamuttu, Johan, *The Dilemma of Independence: Two Decades of Malaysia's Foreign Policy, 1957–1977*, Penang, Universiti Sains Press, 1983.

Saravanamuttu, Johan, The Southeast Asian Development Phenomenon Revisited: From Flying Geese to Lame Ducks?, *Pacifica Review* 10(2), 1998, 111–126.

Sasaki, Hiroshi (ed.), *Higashi Ajia Kyosei no Joken (Conditions for Co-prosperity in East Asia)*, Tokyo, Seshikishobo, 2006, 172–176.

Sato, Toyoshi (ed.), *Higashi Ajia Kyodotai no Kanousei: Nicchu Kankei no Saikento (The Possibility of the East Asian Community: The Re-examination of the Sino-Japanese Relations)*, Tokyo, Ochanomizu Shobo, 2006.

Seethi, K. M. and Vijayan P., Political Economy of India's Third World Policy, in *Engaging with the World: Critical Reflections on India's Foreign Policy* (eds.), Rajen Harshe and K. M. Seethi, 47–69, New Delhi, Orient Longman, 2005.

Senate of the Philippines, North Rail Project Faltering Due to Non-Compliance with Rules — Pimentel, Press Release, 14 July 2008 in the Senate of the Philippines, 14th Congress website [downloaded on 27 October 2008]. Available at http://www.senate.gov.ph/press_release/2008/0714_pimentel1.asp.

Sharma, Ashok B., India, Philippines sign 9 bilateral deals, 5 October 2007, in the Financial Express (India)/bilaterals.org [downloaded on 2 November 2008]. Available at http://www.bilaterals.org/article.php3?id_article=9867.

Shaw, Timothy M., The Non-Aligned Movement and the New International Economic Order, in *Transforming the World Economy?*, Herb Addo, (ed.) Tokyo, United Nations Publications, 1999.

Sheng, Lijun, China–ASEAN Free Trade Area: Origins, Developments, and Strategic Motivations, ISEAS Working Paper: International Politics & Security Issues Series No. 1, 2003, 6–7.

Shirk, Susan, *China: Fragile Power*, Oxford, New York, Oxford University Press, 2007.

Singh, Uday Bhanu, Recent Developments in Myanmar, 2 November 2007 in the IDSA Strategic Comments, Institute for Defense Studies & Analyses website [downloaded on 18 August 2008]. Available at http://www.idsa.in/publications/stratcomments/UdaiBhanuSingh021107.htm.

Sokolsky R., *et al.*, *The Role of Southeast Asia in U.S. Strategy Toward China*, Rand, 2003, 29–42.

Solomon, Jay, Charles Hutzler and Zahid Hussain, China Steps Up Diplomatic Role, 8 December 2003 in the *Wall Street Journal*, US, WSJ, 2003.

Storey, Ian, Burma's Relations with China: Neither Puppet Nor Pawn, in China Brief website, 7(3), (7 February 2007) [downloaded on 18 August 2008]. Available at http://www.jamestown.org/china_brief/article.php?articleid=2373268.

Stuart-Fox, M., *A Short History of China and Southeast Asia*, Allen & Unwin, 2003.

Stuart-Fox, M., Southeast Asia and China: The Role of History and Culture in Shaping Future Relations, *Contemporary Southeast* Asia, 26(1) 2004, 116–139.

Stubbs, Richard, *Rethinking Asia's Economic Miracle: The Political Economy of War, Prosperity an Crisis,* Houndmills, Basingstoke: Palgrave Macmillan, 2005.

Srivastava, Sadhana and Ramkishen S. Rajan, What Does the Economic Rise of China Imply for ASEAN and India?: Focus on Trade and Investment Flows, in Freewebs.com [downloaded on 8 March 2006]. Available at www.freewebs.com/rrajan01/Keha_ch09.pdf, pp. 1–34.

Sutter, R., Asia in the Balance: America and China's 'Peaceful Rise', *Current History* 2004, 284–289.

Sutter, Robert Sutter, *China's Rise in Asia: Promises and Perils,* Lanham, Md., Rowman and Littlefield, 2005.

Tanaka, Akihiko, *Ajia no Nakano Nippon (Japan in Asia),* Tokyo, NTT Shuppan, 2007, 232.

The Nation, China's appeal overshadows US, 29 June 2004 in *The Nation,* 6B.

Tkacik, J., A Chinese Military Superpower?, 8 March 2007 webmemo#1389, in *Heritage Foundation,* unpaginated.

Tkacik, J., Hedging Against China, in *Heritage Foundation* Backgrounder #1925, April 17, 2006.

The Japan Defense Agency (ed.), *Higashi Ajia Senryaku Gaikan 2006, The Survey of the Strategic Situation in East Asia,* 2006, 186–190.

Timmons, Heather, Indians bristle at U.S. criticism on food prices, 13 May 2008 [downloaded on 1 June 2008]. Available at http://www.iht.com/articles/2008/05/13/business/food.php.

Tyler, Ralph J., The future of India–China trade, *The Economic Times,* January 14, 2008.

United Nations Development Programme, *Human Development Report 2007–08, Fighting Climate Change: Human Solidarity in a Divided World* New York, UNDP, 2008.

United Nations, General Assembly, *Declaration of the Establishment of a New International Economic Order, 2229th Plenary Meeting, 1 May,* New York, UN, 1974.

Vatikiotis, M. and M. Hiebert, Free Trade Agreements: China's Tight Embrace, 17 July 2003 in *Far Eastern Economic Review.* Available at www.feer.com.

Veltmeyer, Henry, *New Perspectives on Globalization and Antiglobalization: Prospects for a New World Order?,* Aldershot, Ashgate, 2008.

Vietnam Netbridge, Vietnam, India issue joint declaration on strategic partnership, 7 July 2007 in the VietnamNetBridge, website [downloaded on 18 August 2008]. Available at http://english.vietnamnet.vn/politics/2007/07/715169/.

Vohra, Subhash, China and India are Rising Economic Powers, in News VoA.com, 9 April 2007. Available at http://www.voanews.com.

Wadhva, Charan, India 2020: Comparative Positioning of India and China, in *Rising Powers: Event Report Abstract of Presentation*, London, Foreign Policy Centre, 2005.

Wain, B., Free trade: Nothing's Free, 31 October 2002, in *Far Eastern Economic Review*. Available at www.feer.com.

Wallerstein, Immanuel, Incorporation of Indian subcontinent into capitalist world economy, *Economic and Political Weekly*, XXI 25(4) January 1986, pp. 28–39.

Wanandi, Jusuf, ASEAN and China Form Strategic Partnership, 15 Dec 2005 in the Jakarta Post. Available at http://taiwansecurity.org/News/2005/JP-151205.htm.

Wang Jianwei: *Limited Adversaries: Post-Cold War Sino-American Mutual Images*, New York, Oxford University Press, 2000.

Wong, Kan Seng, Continuity and change in Singapore's Foreign Policy, 15 November 1988 [Speech by Mr Wong Kan Seng, Minister for Foreign Affairs and Minister for Community Development, to the Singapore Press Club on 15 November 1988 at 12.30 pm at Les Oiseaux, Marina Mandarin].

World Bank, China Quarterly Update June 2008, in the Washington, DC World Bank website. Available at http://www.worldbank.org/.

World Trade Organization, International trade and tariff data, China, in Geneva WTO website. Available at http://stat.wto.org/CountryProfile/WSDBCountryPFView.aspx?Language=E&Country=CN.

World Trade Organization, International trade and tariff data, India, 2008 in the Geneva WTO website. Available at http://stat.wto.org/CountryProfile/WSDBCountryPFView.aspx?Language=E&Country=IN.

Zakaria, Ali, Normalization of Relations with China, in Fauziah Mohammad Taib (ed.), *Number One Wisma Putra*, Kuala Lumpur, Institute of Diplomacy and Foreign Relations, 2006, 119–130.

Zhao, Hong, India and China: Rivals or Partners in Southeast Asia?, *Journal of Contemporary Southeast Asia*, 29(1), 2007, 126–127.

Index

Abdullah administration, 71
Abridged Realism, 117, 121
African–Asian–Latin American
    countries, 28
Albanian resolution, 62
American Financial Crisis, 142
American political and security
    commitment, 114
Amin, Samir, 23
Anglo–Japanese Alliance Treaty, 90
Antrix Corporation Ltd., 73
APEC forum, 42
Arroyo, 46, 48
    administration, 49–50
ASEAN
    activism, 106
    Chinese strategy, 138–140
ASEAN Charter, 55
ASEAN-China and ASEAN-India
    frameworks
    bilateral, 54
ASEAN–China Closer Economic
    Relations, 108
ASEAN–China collaboration, 120
ASEAN–China Comprehensive
    Economic Cooperation, 40
ASEAN–China Eminent Persons
    Group (EPG), 114

ASEAN–China EPG, 123
ASEAN–China FTA, 136, 138, 140,
    144
ASEAN–China relations, 49
ASEAN–China strategic partnership,
    120
ASEAN–China trade, 136
ASEAN claimant, 49
ASEAN–India Declaration on
    Cooperation to Combat
    International Terrorism, 120
ASEAN–India partnership, 120
ASEAN–Japan trade, 136
ASEAN Plus Three and East Asia
    Community building projects, 49
ASEAN Plus Three Summit, 40, 108
ASEAN regional forum (ARF), 54,
    56, 105, 119, 121
ASEAN regional institutions, 108
ASEAN states (Cambodia, Laos,
    Myanmar, Thailand, and
    Vietnam), 42
ASEAN's Treaty of Amity and
    Cooperation, 16
ASEAN summit
    in Bangkok, 109
ASEAN–US trade, 136
Asia–Europe Meeting (ASEM), 42

Asian civilization(s), 59
Asian Common Market, 68
Asian Drama
    An Inquiry into the Poverty of
        Nations, 1
Asian economic and political
    ascendancy, 60
Asian Monetary Fund, 84
Asian subcontinental power, 65
Asia–Pacific Economic Cooperation
    (APEC), 69, 84, 113
Asia-Pacific countries, 99, 105
Asia, rise of
    negotiating the rise, 59–77
    non-proliferation efforts, 94
Association of Southeast Asian
    Nations (ASEAN), 65

Baginda, Razak, 70
Bandung spirit, 26
"Beijing Consensus", 132
Beijing Olympics, 2008, 18
Beijing Summer Olympics, 1
BIMSTEC (Bangladesh, India,
    Myanmar, Sri Lanka, Thailand
    Economic Cooperation), 42
BJP-led National Democratic
    Alliance (NDA), 34
Bollywood's ability, 124
Burmese refugees, 54
Bush administration, 135
Bush, George W., 3

Can Asians Think?, 109
"Charm diplomacy", 44
Chicago Council on Global
    Affairs
    World Public Opinion in 2007,
        45

China and India, rise of, 39–57
    competition for influence and
        regional power rivalry, 40–44
    geo-political narratives from
        Singapore perspective, 99–125
    imaging, 40–44
    implications for Southeast Asia,
        39–57, 127–144
    Japanese perspective on, 79–97
    look east policy, 1980s–1990s,
        67–69
    Philippine perspective, 39–57
    positioning towards, 61–67
    Singapore perspective, 99–125
    "soft power" capabilities, 50–53
    Thai perspective, 127–144
China–ASEAN Free Trade Area
    (CAFTA), 40–41, 140
China–ASEAN relations, 137–139
China–ASEAN summit, 138
"China fever", 133
China–India ascendancy
    managing, 71–76
China, rise of
    ASEAN and, 44–57
    China ahead of India, 44–50
    conflict in East Asia, 11–19
    constructivism approach, 17–18
    cultural influence, 43
    cultural power, 131–33
    "dual identities", 17
    economic growth rate of, 24
    economic power, 130–131
    foreign direct investments and
        financial assistance, 48
    grand strategy, 133–134
    institutionalization approach,
        14–16
    its implications to Asia, 128–134

Japanese investment in, 81
maoism in, 12
military power, 130
realist approach, 11–14
relations with the philippines,
  44–50
system of military alliances
  against, 13
uncertain development of, 18–19
valorisation of, 23
Yunnan province, 43
China's aggression, 103
China's Foreign Ministry, 70
China's ICT sector,
China-inspired Malayan Communist
  Party, 62
China–US economic competition
  in Southeast Asia, 135–136
China–US political and security
  competition
  in Southeast Asia, 136–137
China–Vietnam rivalry, 67
Chindia, 141–142
Chinese diplomacy, 16
Chinese economic growth, 18
Chinese economy today, 2, 128
Chinese IR community, 6
Chinese policy in Southeast Asia, 104
Chinese pro-active diplomacy, 139
Clash of Civilizations, 59
CLMV (Cambodia, Laos, Myanmar
  and Vietnam), 40–41
Cold War, 16, 83, 90, 133
The Coming Collapse of China, 100
Comprehensive Economic
  Cooperation Agreement (CECA)
  India–Thailand, 41
Congress-led United Progressive
  Alliance (UPA), 34

Constructivism approach, 17–18
Council for Security Cooperation in
  the Asia–Pacific (CSCAP), 102
CTBT treaty
  UN-adopted, 93
Cultural Revolution, 1

Declaration on Conduct
  in the South China Sea, 16
Defense White Paper of Japan,
  95–96
Democratic Action Party (DAP), 72
Deng Xiaoping's
  dictum, 14
  pragmatic wisdom, 124
Die Zeit, 110
Diplomatically distant, 119
"Dual identities", 17

East Asia
  development of multilateral
    institutions and frameworks
    in East Asia, 83–86
  multi-polarity in, 90
  Washington's hegemony in, 12
East Asia Summit (EAS), 41, 56, 86,
  115
East Asian Economic Caucus
  (EAEC), 68–69
East Asian Economic Grouping
  (EAEG), 68
East Asian international orders, 87
East Asian politics, 87
East–West
  dissonance, 110
  perspectives, 110
Economic Advisory Council (EAC),
  30
Economic competition, 142

Economic gap, 92
Economic interests, 40–43
The Economic Outlook for 2008–09,
    30
Electronic and electrical (E&E)
    industry, 75
Economy, top 10 countries, 2
English-speaking population, 88
Enhanced economic chances
        for Japan, 80–82
European military alliances, 105
'Exclusive beneficiaries', 29
Export and Import Bank of China,
    47

Filipinos, 45
Food Action Nippon Movement, 91
Foreign direct investment (FDI),
    128–129, 131
        in the world, 24, 75
Foreign Investment
        in approved projects in Malaysia
        (2002–2006), 75
Free trade agreement (FTA), 40–42
    negotiations, 85

GATT, 28
        Uruguay Round negotiations, 84
GDP, 24, 30, 128, 130
        growth rate of India, 30
        non-farm sector, 30
        of Japan, 88
Geographic proximity
        with China, 44
Geopolitical competition, 142–143
Germany and Japan in
    World War II, 13
Germany in World War I, 13
Gilpin, Robert, 60

Global trade mechanism, 28
Graziano Transmissioni, 4
Great Depression, 36
Greater Chinese societies, 101
Greater East Asian Co-prosperity
    Sphere, 84
Greater Mekong Subregion (GMS),
    43

"Hegemonic stability", 60
HINDRAF leaders, 66
Hindu–Muslim divide, 124
Hiroshima and Nagasaki
    experiences, 94
Hitler's Germany and imperial
    Japan, 15
Hobbesian struggle
        zero-sum, 14
Hu Jintao, 32, 35
*The Human Development Report
    2007–08*, 29
Human Poverty Index (HDI), 29–30
"Human Rights and Human
    Responsibilities", 110
Humanitarian contingent, 49

Ikenberry, John, 15
IMF, 28
IMF-World Bank combine, 28
IMF World Bank-WTO triad, 28
Impasse in Myanmar
        breaking, 54
India and China
        'Asian century', 22
        'current 'success stories', 22
        development trajectories, 22–26
        developmental problems and
            challenges, 5
        differences between, 3

economic power status, 26
emerging, 21–37
future of, 7–9
good governance for, 8
growth rates of, 23
'impressive economic growth',
  22
in new 'Asian Century', 32
Malaysia's relations with, 59–77
population, 4
potentials and constraints,
  21–37
US superpower deal, 8
Western traditional
  international relations (IR)
  approaches, 5
India–ASEAN Summit, 119
India-China relations, 32
India–Japan Study Group Report, 81
Indian pharmaceutical companies,
  46
Indian Railway Construction Co
  (IRCON), 72
Indian Technical and Economic
  Cooperation (ITEC), 70
India–Pakistani nuclear
  development competition, 96
India, rise of
  challenges, 26–32
  Chindia, 141–142
  comparing rise of China and
    India, 140–141
  economic competition, 142
  economy, 24
  emerging, 26–32
  GDP growth rate of, 30
  geopolitical competition,
    142–143
  long-term rival in South Asia, 33

Malaysia's relations with, 65
military competition, 143
partiality to the Soviet Union,
  67
social welfare/security agenda
  of, 28
India's controversial patent law, 46
India's obligations, 28
Institutionalization approach,
  14–16
Intra-regional normative ASEAN
  Way, 118
Ishihara, Shintaro, 59

Japanese constitution
  Article Nine of, 83
Japanese investments, 81
Japanese Ministry of Defense, 80
Japanese Ministry of Foreign
  Affairs, 97
"The Japanese miracle", 68
Japanese public school education
  Hiroshima and Nagasaki
    experiences, 94
Japanese self-food-supply ratio, 91
Japanese–Indian common study
  report, 82
Japanese–Indian summit, 82
Jawaharlal Nehru Award for
  International Understanding, 66
JETRO website, 81
Jihadis terrorists, 4
Joint Marine Seismic Understanding
  (JMSU), 50

Kagan, Robert, 12
Kennedy, Paul
  The Rise and Fall of the Great
    Powers, 12

Koh, Tommy, 104, 111–116
    East–West misunderstanding,
      110
    institution-building emphasis,
      116
    pragmatism, 113
Koizumi's administration, 85
Kuala Lumpur Declaration, 65
Kuantan Doctrine, 67

Labuan, Mitco, 73
Langkawi International Maritime
    and Aerospace (LIMA), 71
Leifer, Michael, 102–103, 121
    balance-of-power, 105
    engagement within a regional
      order, 123
"Let sleeping dogs lie", 110
Liberal Democratic Party, 83
Liberal institutionalization, 14
The Little Red Dot, 113
'Look East policy', 32, 67–69

Mahathir, 71
Mahbubani, Kishore, 59, 109
    East–West tract, 109
Malayan Communist Party (MCP),
    63–64
Malayan Voice of Revolution, 63
Malaysia–Indian Defence
    Cooperation Meetings (MIDCOM),
    70
Malaysia–India relations, 62, 66
Malaysian–ASEAN scheme, 65
Malaysian economy, 73
Malaysian military personnel, 70
Malaysian Mining Corporation
    (MMC), 71

Malaysian nationality, 64
    "internal problem", 64
Malaysia's large Chinese population,
    72
Malaysia's overall trade, 75
Manmohan Singh, 3, 33, 73, 82
Maoist revolutionary state, 17
Maoist-inspired Naxalites, 4
Marxism, 12
Marxist–Leninist–Maoism, 12
Marxist–Maoist legacy, 13
Mearsheimer, John, 132
Middle Kingdom, 13
MILAN, 71
Military competition, 143
Millennium Development Goals, 100
Mischief Reef, 70, 103
Mohamad, Mahathir, 59, 67
"Monroe Doctrine", 132
Muslim-majority countries, 137
Myrdal, Karl Gunnar, 1

National Association of Software and
    Service Companies (NASSCOM),
    36
National Defence College, 71
National Democratic Alliance
    (NDA), 34
National Institute of Defense
    Studies (NIDS), 44
National Socialist Council of
    Nagaland, 53
Naxalite uprisings, 31
Nehru government, 27
New Asian drama, 1–9
New International Economic Order
    (NIEO), 27
Non-aligned movement (NAM), 26

Non-ASEAN powers, 109
Non-compliance with Rules —
  Pimentel, 48
Non-East Asian powers, 116
Non-traditional security (NTS), 44,
  54
    exploring cooperation in, 53–54
    problems, 54
Norm building and East Asia
  community, 55–56
North Korean nuclear issue, 85, 94
North Korean regime, 4
North Rail Project Faltering, 48
North Rail rehabilitation project,
  47–48
North-South axis, 27
North-South dialogue, 36
NPT dominos, 93
Nuclear non-proliferation treaty
  (NPT), 80
    systems, 93–94, 96

One-China policy, 18, 104
Onn, Hussein, 66

"Pan-Asian Railway" project, 43
"Peaceful rise", 134
Pacific War, 83
PASSEX, 71
People's Republic of China, 12,
  62–65, 102
Perbadanan Nasional or National
  Corporation, 62
Philippine
    China ties, 49
    Congress, 49
    military, 49
    perspective, 39–57

Philippines–China trade value, 47
Philippines–India trade value, 47
Philippines vis-à-vis China and
  India, 44
Phnom Penh, 40
PINR (Power and Interest News
  Report), 52
Political instability
    widening economic gap, 92–93
Pokhran-II nuclear tests, 43
Policy of open regionalism, 120
Post Cold War context, 103, 108
Post-Mao Era, 14
Post-US hegemony, 87
Post World War I, 90
Pragmatism, 60, 117
Premier Wen Jabao, 46
Public Administration Medal (Gold),
  109
Purchasing power parity (PPP)
    calculations, 2, 21, 130–131

Ramos, Fidel V, 49
Razak government, 65
Regional power rivalry, 43–47
The Rise of China and India, 79
Royal Malaysian Air Force (RMAF),
  71
Russo–Chinese–Indian military
  triangle, 95–97

Save Democracy Fund, 62
Self Defense Forces, 83
Shanghai Cooperation Organization
  (SCO), 54
'Shared Vision for the 21st Century',
  33
Shirk, Susan, 19

Singaporean leadership, 105
Singapore-centric perspectives, 99
Singapore's Chinese-majority's affiliation with China, 101
Singapore's diplomats,
Singapore's foreign policy, 101, 114, 116–117, 123
Singapore's geo-strategic thinking, 115
Singapore's sense, 102
Sino-centric system, 13–14
Sino–Indian competition in Southeast Asia, 143–144
Sino–Japanese
   relations, 85
   trade, 92
Sino–U.S.
   conflict, 13, 132
   rivalry, 94–95
Social development indicators, 29
Socialist Party, 83
Socio-economic gap, 80
"Soft power", 44
   capabilities, 50–53
Southeast Asia
   and East Asia, 44
   Mekong states, 43
   neighbors, 51
   people, 65
Southeast Asian Nuclear Weapons Free Zone (SEANWFZ), 65, 136, 139
Southeast Asian politics and international relations, 102
South-South cooperation, 36
Study Group Report, 81
Suara Revolusi Malaya, 63

Sub-Committee for Military Cooperation (SCMC), 70
Swallow Reef, 70

Taiwan's political aspirations, 104
Tata industrial group, 4
Terumbu Layang Layang, 70
Third India–ASEAN Summit, 41
Third World countries
   mobilising, 26
Three concerns
   environmental burdens, 90–92
   Japan passing or nothing, 88–90
   political instability as a result of widening economic gap, 92–93
Three threats
   NPT dominos, 93–94
   Russo–Chinese–Indian military triangle, 95–97
   Sino–US rivalry, 94–95
Treaty of Amity and Cooperation (TAC), 119
   in Southeast Asia, 85, 136–137

UNDP Human Development Report, 29
UNDP's China Human Development Report 2005, 25
UN General Assembly, 27
United Liberation Front of Asom, 53
United National Liberation Front, 53
United Nations Conference on Trade and Development (UNCTAD), 26
United Nations Convention on the Law of Sea (UNCLOS), 50
United Progressive Alliance (UPA), 34

The United States and East Asia, 113

UN Security Council, 109

U.S.–Chinese power transition, 15

US hegemony
balancer role between China and India, 86–88

US–Japan alliance system, 89

U.S.–Japan relations
in the Asia-Pacific region, 87

US–Japan
security alliance, 88, 90
Security system, 95
Security Treaty System, 89

US–Japanese Security Treaty, 83, 89

US-led industrialised countries, 28

US nuclear umbrella, 94

US-Sino rivalry, 135

Vedanta and Hindalco companies, 142

Venecia, Jose De, 48

Vietnamese invasion
of Cambodian, 108

Vietnam War, 67

The Voice of Asia, 59

"Washington Consensus"
US-inspired, 132

Washington Treaty system, 90

Western international relations
theory, 13

Western IR scholars, 5

White Paper of Japan, 95

World Bank, 28

World Trade Organisation (WTO), 28, 31, 41, 80, 108

Yoshida doctrine, 83

Zero-sum game or balance, 39

Zone of Peace and Neutrality in Southeast Asia, 65

Zone of Peace Freedom and Neutrality (ZOPFAN), 65

ZTE national broadband, 48